PAST INTO PRESENT 1

43 AD–1400

PAST INTO PRESENT 1

43 AD–1400

Christopher Culpin
David Linsell

Series Editor:
Martin Booth

COLLINS
EDUCATIONAL

COLLINS LOWER SCHOOL HISTORY

CONTENTS

FINDING OUT ABOUT...
THE ROMANS IN BRITAIN

SOURCE 1 Hadrian's Wall

SOURCE 2 Roman road in Leicestershire

Y OU CAN TELL that the Romans once lived in Britain from the huge works they left behind, like Sources 1 and 2. Hadrian's Wall runs for 80 miles across Northern England. It is 4 metres high, and wide enough to walk on. There are several sections of Roman road, like Source 2, still in use. They may now be lanes, or tracks, or even main roads. They are all more or less straight, so you can easily spot them on a map.

Of course, the Romans left behind smaller objects, too, like the mirror in Source 3. Objects like this mirror prove that history is not a fairy story; the Romans were real people who used real objects that we can see and touch. That is why there are lots of SOURCES in this book— sources of EVIDENCE to show us where we get our information from. In fact the mirror is a source of many different kinds of evidence. It is evidence that the Romans were skilled at making things in silver. It is evidence that they liked objects decorated with flowers. It is evidence that some Romans at least cared what they looked like. Is it evidence that they wore make-up?

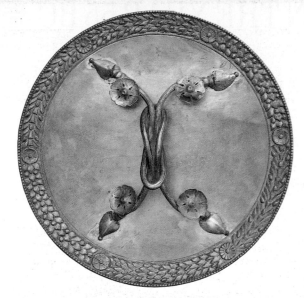

SOURCE 3 You can see this mirror in the Rowley's House Museum, Shrewsbury

Tombstones, like Source 4, are also sources which tell us quite a lot about the Romans. This one gives us evidence about the clothes the Romans wore, their families, and their writing. Can you think of any other kinds of evidence you can get from this source?

The people who study objects from the past and help us to understand them are called ARCHAEOLOGISTS. Archaeologists often have only a ruin, or a few pieces of an object, to work from. Sometimes they make a reconstruction, or a model, to show what they think it used to look like. Source 5 is a model of what they think the Roman palace at Fishbourne, Sussex may have looked like.

SOURCE 4 Tombstone from the Yorkshire Museum at York

From the five sources shown here, what do we *know about the Romans, for certain*?
From these sources, what else seems *likely to be true about the Romans*?

SOURCE 5 Roman palace at Fishbourne, Sussex

AIMS

In this unit we shall be finding out about the Romans. We shall find out where the Romans came from and what Britain was like when they arrived. We shall begin to learn how historians find out about people from the past. We shall see how archaeologists use different sources of evidence to find out what they were like and how they lived. In history, we need to be precise about when things happened. We shall, therefore, look at how dates are calculated.

ROMANS AND CELTS IN THE YEAR 55 BC

Time

Years are counted from the birth of Christ. Years after this should have the letters AD (anno domini)—Latin for 'in the year of Our Lord'. Years before Christ have the letters BC—before Christ. We count the years BC backwards as every year that passed was nearer the birth of Christ. So the year after 88 BC was 87 BC. A century is a hundred years. The 1st century was from the birth of Christ to 100 AD.

The Romans

The city of Rome is in Italy. It was founded in the 8th century BC. The Romans had a powerful and well-disciplined army, as we shall see. By the beginning of the 1st century BC they had taken over all the other towns, cities and people in Italy.

By 55 BC they were fighting to take over Northern France (see Source 6). Their great general, Julius Caesar, was in command. He thought that his enemies were getting food and weapons from the people of Britain. He

hardly knew anything about Britain, so he began to ask questions. Some traders went to Britain regularly. He wrote down what they told him in the book he was writing about his wars.

> **SOURCE 7**
>
> 'The population is very large; they have many houses and large herds of animals. Apart from beech and fir, there are trees of every kind. They think it is wrong to eat hares, or chickens or geese, but they breed them as pets. They do not sow corn, but live on milk and meat, and wear clothes made of animal skins. All the Britons, though, dye their skin with woad, which produces a blue colour, and thereby look all the more terrifying in battle.'
>
> Extract from *The war in France* by Julius Caesar

Julius Caesar is describing all the Britons in a few words, as if they were all the same. Does the evidence support his account? We shall find out.

SOURCE 6 Map of Europe in 55 BC

BRITAIN

Rhine

GAUL

Danube

Black Sea

SPAIN

Rome

MACEDONIA

Carthage

SYRIA

Mediterranean Sea

AFRICA

EGYPT

Red Sea

Roman Empire in 55 BC

The Celts

People had been living in Britain for 350,000 years before Julius Caesar. Many different groups had travelled, and settled there. By the time of Julius Caesar the main inhabitants of Britain were what we now call Celts. Whatever language they spoke, it was not written down, so our only sources of evidence about them are the objects they left behind. If we look at some Celtic objects from different parts of Britain we can begin to get some idea of what the Celts were like.

SOURCE 10 Spinning equipment (weights) from Somerset

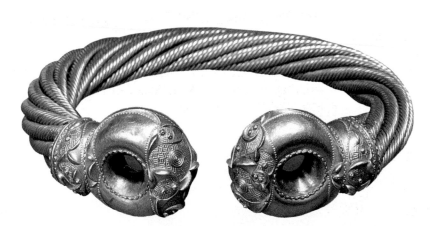

SOURCE 8 Quern used for grinding corn into flour, from Orkney

SOURCE 11 Ornamental Shield, found in the Thames

SOURCE 9 Torc (necklet) made of electrum (gold and silver) from Norfolk

Sometimes archaeologists find a place where Celtic people lived. They can tell where the hut was, from the holes in the ground where the posts were. They can then build a new hut to see what it might have looked like. Source 12 shows one of these reconstructions.

SOURCE 12 Farmstead, in Hampshire, reconstructed. From the size of the hut, archaeologists think that it was lived in by a large family group of about 15–20 people.

1 Which skills and crafts do the Celts seem to have been good at?
2 What kind of decoration did they seem to like?
3 Some of the objects the archaeologists have found show that Julius Caesar, in Source 7, was not correct in some of the things he wrote about Britain. Which objects tell us this?
4 Why do you think he made these mistakes?

Celtic Britain had no main roads or cities. Quite a lot of the countryside was farmed, and there were many small villages. The people also hunted wild animals and fished in the lakes. As we saw from Source 12, their houses were not very grand. Nevertheless, they had some beautifully-made and decorated objects, like the torc (Source 9).

Britain did not have one ruler and one government, as it does now. Each area had its own chief or ruler. These people lived quite well, trading wool, lead and tin from Britain for wine from France. The shield (Source 11) probably belonged to one of these local chiefs. Wars between these chiefs were common. Huge hill-forts were built as protection for the families and animals if a rival army invaded the area.

SOURCE 13 Maiden Castle—an example of a huge hill-fort

In pairs.
1 In this source find:
   a The large open area in the middle, where huts were built and animals grazed.
   b The ditches and ramparts. In this case there are four successive layers to get through. These also kept enemy archers and slingers at a distance.
   c The twisting entrance track at the end. Attackers would find it difficult to find the way in.
2 a What evidence do we find in this source about the number of people needed to build Maiden Castle?
   b What does this source tell you about the skill and power of the local chief?

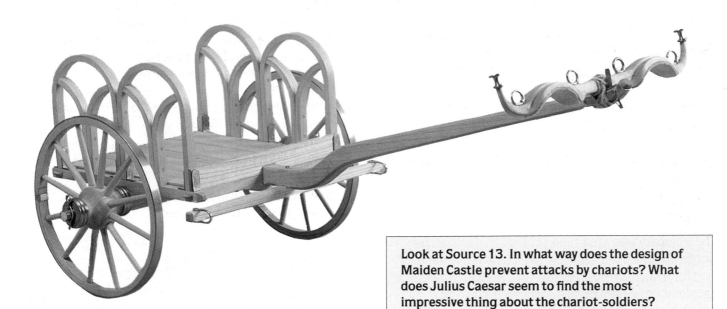

Look at Source 13. In what way does the design of Maiden Castle prevent attacks by chariots? What does Julius Caesar seem to find the most impressive thing about the chariot-soldiers?

SOURCE 14 Model of Celtic war-chariot. This is another reconstruction by archaeologists. They used pictures from Roman coins, and the remains of some parts of the chariots which they found as clues.

The Celts were fierce fighters too. They fought on foot, on horseback, and from chariots.

Julius Caesar described in his book how these chariots were used:

SOURCE 15

'They begin by driving all over the field hurling javelins. The terror inspired by the horses and the noise of the wheels is usually enough to throw the enemy ranks into disorder. Their skill, which they learn from endless training and practice, may be judged by the fact that they can control their horses at full gallop on the steepest slope, stop and turn them in a moment, run along the pole, stand on the yoke and get back again into the chariot as quick as lightning.'

Julius Caesar wrote Source 15 from personal experience. In 55 BC he decided to have a look at Britain for himself, and set off with an army of 10,000 men. He landed in Kent, but the ships carrying his cavalry were blown off course, and couldn't land. He found that the Celts were fierce and dangerous fighters, especially when the Romans were at a disadvantage, such as during their landing on the beach. He also learned that Britain was a prosperous country, which would be a valuable addition to the growing Roman Empire. However, with no cavalry he dared not stay too long, and returned to France after three weeks.

In the following year, 54 BC, he returned, with a bigger army. This time he stayed for nearly three months. He marched inland, and crossed the Thames, defeating the Celts several times. His disciplined soldiers were too strong for the Celts, but they would not give in to him. It was not going to be easy to conquer Britain, and he returned to France.

For nearly a hundred years the Romans left Britain alone, while they conquered other lands. The Celtic leaders had mixed feelings about this huge Empire just across the Channel.

Some admired the Romans and tried to get on with them. Others hated, envied or feared the Romans.

In 43 AD some of the local chiefs in England were fighting among themselves. One was driven out of his lands, and called on the Roman Emperor for help. The Emperor, Claudius, decided that this was a good opportunity to win Britain for the Roman Empire. He sent a large army to conquer Britain.

The Roman Army

Source 16 shows a legionary, the main type of Roman soldier.

> 1 **Which parts of his body are protected by armour?**
> 2 **What are his three main fighting weapons?**
> 3 **What does he wear on his feet?**

The legionary was a full-time, professional soldier. He signed up for 25 years, on low pay, but was given enough land for a farm when he retired. Only Roman citizens, not people who the Romans had conquered, could be legionaries. A man called Josephus, who fought against the Romans in Palestine in AD 67 explains why the Roman army was hardly ever defeated:

SOURCE 17

'As if born holding swords in their hands they never rest from training. Their training is as strenuous as real warfare. Every soldier, every day, exercises as eagerly as if he were in action. That is why they make light of fighting. No confusion drives them out of their usual formation. They are not paralysed with fear or exhausted by hard work. Victory is inevitable, for their enemies can never equal them.'

4,800 legionaries together with some cavalry made up a legion. Each legion had a number.

Claudius' army had four legions, the 2nd, 9th, 14th and 20th. In addition there were other soldiers, cavalry, artillery (firing the ballista—a machine like a huge catapult) cooks, blacksmiths, carpenters, road-builders etc.—40,000 men in all.

> **Compare Sources 14, 15, 16 and 17. Who do you think would win in battle, the Celts or the Romans? Give reasons for your answer.**

Some of the local chiefs welcomed the Romans. The Romans did not usually interfere with local rulers, as long

SOURCE 16 Full size figure of a legionary, from Chester Museum, wearing modern replicas of Roman armour and weapons.

as they accepted Roman rule, paid taxes to Rome, and did what they were told. One Celtic chief, Cogidubnus, immediately accepted Roman rule. He was made a king,. and, with Roman help, built a huge palace at Fishbourne, in Sussex (see Source 5, page 7).

You can see that there were big advantages in co-operating with the Romans. Not all the Celtic rulers gave in without a fight, however. By one of the gates of Maiden Castle (Source 13) archaeologists have found these bones:

SOURCE 18 Skull smashed by a sword-blow

SOURCE 19 Ballista bolt embedded in the spine of a Celtic warrior

> **What do these sources tell us about Celtic resistance to the Romans?**

The Roman armies were victorious everywhere they went and by 47 AD the whole of southern and eastern England was under their control. They made their capital at Colchester. Later they began the slower and more difficult business of conquering Wales, western and northern England.

Boudica's Revolt

In 60 AD the Roman army was fighting in Anglesey when news came of a rebellion by the Iceni, a tribe who lived in part of East Anglia. There were several reasons for the rebellion. The Iceni objected to the Roman religion, which seemed to insult their own gods. They did not like the fact that retired legionaries had been given some of their land. The last straw came when the king of the Iceni died. The Romans began to seize all his land and possessions. When his widow, Boudica, protested, she was whipped. This was the final insult to the proud Iceni who regarded Boudica as their queen. The Iceni rebelled in protest.

Before the Roman army could return from Wales, Boudica and her people had sacked and burnt the Roman towns of Colchester, St Albans and London. Any Romans they found were immediately killed. A Roman writer described Boudica:

SOURCE 20

'She was a tall woman with piercing eyes and a loud voice. A great mass of red hair hung down to below her waist. Round her neck was a large gold torc. She wore a full, flowing tartan dress, and over it a thick cloak, fastened by a brooch.'

The Roman legions marched rapidly south to meet Boudica and her followers. Boudica spoke to her soldiers before the battle:

SOURCE 21

'We British are used to women commanders in war. I am not fighting as an ordinary person for my lost freedom, my bruised body and my outraged daughters. The gods will grant us the revenge we deserve. . . . Think how many of you there are, and why we are fighting; then you will win this battle, or die. That is what I, a woman, plan to do—let the men live in slavery, if they want!'

However, once again the Roman legions triumphed over the Celts. Many of Boudica's followers were killed. She herself took poison to avoid being captured. The revolt was over.

From then on the Romans made more of an effort to win over the British. For the next 350 years Britain was a quiet and usually peaceful part of the Roman Empire. Let us see what Britain was like during those years.

ROMAN SETTLEMENT

Towns

Most Roman towns had much the same layout, so we can take examples from different parts of the country.

SOURCE 22 Imaginary aerial view of the Roman town of St Albans

> Look closely at Source 22.
> 1 Describe the plan of the streets.
> 2 How is the town protected from attack?
> 3 How many gates are there?
> 4 How do you think the artist knew how to draw the reconstruction in Source 22?

SOURCE 23 Finds from St Albans

Near the centre of the town in Source 22 is an open square with a large building down one side of it. What can this be? Source 23 gives us some clues. These objects were found in the building. The wooden boards contained a thin layer of soft wax. This could be written on using the 'stylus' (the object like a pen). The boards were then closed and tied with string. A blob of sealing wax was melted over the lamp and dropped on to the knot. The seal was then pressed into the wax.

After the message had been sent and read, the boards would be warmed to melt the wax. They could then be used again.

This building was a place where writing and official business took place. It acted as the council offices and law courts, and was called the 'basilica'.

In front of the basilica was an open square, the 'forum'. The forum in a Roman town was a place where people could meet and talk. All round the forum were shops. These were much the same sorts of shops as we have today. Here are some carvings of scenes in shops. These are from Italy, but shops in Britain would have been like this too.

SOURCE 24 Shop A

SOURCE 25 Shop B

The Romans didn't have pubs selling beer, but wine shops selling wine. The jar in Source 26 has the address of the wine shop scratched on to it—'London, next door to the Temple of Isis'.

SOURCE 26
Wine-jar from a London wine shop

1 What is for sale in shops A and B?
2 Of the four people on the left in shop A, two are rich customers, and two are their slaves. Which is which? How can you tell?
3 In Shop B find the scales for weighing out the goods.

1 What does this tell us about trade between London and the wine-growing parts of Europe in Roman times?

Leisure

One of the favourite activities of the Romans was to go to the baths. These were large buildings with many rooms. The visitor undressed and went straight into a room with a cold bath. Next came a heated room, followed by a very hot room. The bather sweated a lot and went into another warm room. Olive oil was rubbed on the body, and the oil, sweat and dirt scraped off. You then got into a large warm bath. People might spend hours here, sitting around, talking to friends, eating snacks or swimming. When it was time to go, you returned to the cold room for a cold dip before getting dressed.

SOURCE 27 Roman baths in Bath

Explain the ways that the Romans made this bath look grand and imposing.

You can see that going to the baths was partly to keep clean, partly to keep fit and partly as a social activity. Rich people had their own baths, but every town had one or more public baths.

Other forms of leisure activity were visiting the theatre or going to see sporting events in an amphitheatre. Source 28 shows a reconstruction of the amphitheatre at Caerleon, the main army town in South Wales.

SOURCE 28 Reconstruction of the amphitheatre at Caerleon

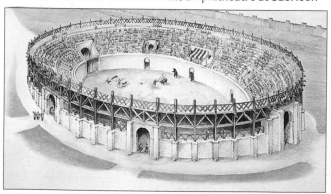

Various events took place here—wrestling, circuses, acrobatics, bear-baiting and gladiators fighting. One gladiator had full armour and weapons, the other only a net and a long three-pointed spear, the trident. They often fought to the death.

Homes

As in Britain today, there were some large houses and some small. Most were only single-storey, and most people lived in only one or two rooms. The rich, however, had large comfortable houses. In fact they lived at a standard never seen in Britain before, and not seen again in many ways until the 20th century.

Large houses had many rooms grouped around a courtyard, like those you can just make out in Source 22. The important rooms had floors covered with mosaic (see Sources 29 and 38). These were tiny pieces of coloured tile, about 1 cm square, arranged to form patterns or pictures. The houses of the better-off Romans also had central heating. This was from a 'hypocaust'. The floor was raised up half a metre on brick columns, as you can see in the top left-hand corner of Source 29, and the air in the space under the floor was heated in a furnace. Hollow bricks were also built into the walls, so warm air could rise up these and heat the walls of the room.

SOURCE 29 Remains of part of a mosaic and a hypocaust from Chedworth

SOURCE 30 A Roman meal-time. The servants can be seen to the left and right with members of the household in the centre.

1 What are the servants doing?

The items used in the house in the kitchen and the dining room were skilfully made too.

SOURCE 31 Bronze saucepan from Nottingham

SOURCE 33 Feeding bottles for children from Colchester

SOURCE 32
Huge silver dish
from Suffolk

SOURCE 34 Glassware from St Albans

2 Compare these items from Roman times with the type of things we use today. Which are similar, and which are different?

3 What conclusions can you draw about
   a Roman craftsmanship?
   b Roman standards of living?

4 Choose two of these objects to illustrate Roman home life. Explain your choice.

ACTIVITY

1 Work in pairs on this activity. One of you has lived for the past seven years in a Roman town. The other is a distant relative, paying a visit to the town from a part of Britain which the Romans haven't reached yet, where you live in a farmstead like the one in Source 12. The town-dweller takes the visitor round the town explaining all that there is to see. Act out, or write down the story of the visit.

2 Work in groups of four or five on this activity. You are Celtic chiefs, used to living in farmsteads like the one in Source 12. It is 63 AD, three years after the defeat of Boudica's revolt in which two of you took part. The Romans invite you to come and live in the town they are building, to govern the area. They will help you build big houses in the town.
Discuss among yourselves what you will do. Then each make your decision and write down your reasons for it.

Roads

Good roads were essential for Roman life in Britain. At first they were needed to get soldiers about the country quickly in case the British rebelled again. We have already seen that Roman roads were straight (Source 2). This is because they were built for marching men. A straight road is the shortest marching distance, and bends break the rhythm of the march. Straight roads also meant that the soldiers could not be ambushed by an enemy hiding round a bend.

As Roman Britain became more peaceful, there were other uses for the roads. There was trade with Europe and between different parts of Britain. Towns also needed large amounts of food, so roads were needed for this traffic too.

Source 35 shows the surface of part of a Roman road in Lancashire. You can see the stones laid by the Romans still in place, and worn by their waggons.

SOURCE 35 Roman road at Blackstone Edge, Lancashire

Countryside

Cities and straight, wide, paved roads were quite new to Britain. Farming, however, changed very little. The towns provided a good market for corn, meat, fruit and vegetables. The army too needed lots of food, wool and leather, although it took all the corn it needed at no charge. The Romans taught the British some better farming methods, such as how to drain the land.

Most farmsteads throughout the Roman period continued to look much like Source 12. A few of the richest farmers did build new houses, in Roman style. These were called villas. Here is a reconstruction of the villa at Lockleys, near St Albans, as it was in about 150 AD. You can see that it has a verandah at the front, and a porch.

In the 4th century, near to towns and roads, some very luxurious villas were built. They had hypocausts, mosaic floors and their own bath-houses. About 70 of these have been found. Here is one from Lullingstone, in Kent.

You can see that even though the main living rooms of the villa are large, it is still a working farm, with barns, pigsties, byres etc.

> **3** List the major features you notice in Sources 36 and 37.
>
> **4** Which feature do you consider to be most important?

This fine mosaic is from the villa in Source 37. You can see that it is designed like a carpet, with pictures in the middle and a patterned border.

> **5** What questions might you as an historian want to ask about this mosaic? Where might you find evidence to help you answer this question?

SOURCE 36 Lockleys Roman villa

1 What are the walls and roof of the villa made of?

2 How many rooms do you think there are inside?

SOURCE 37 Lullingstone Roman Villa (Reconstruction)

SOURCE 38 Mosaic from Lullingstone

The People

The Roman way of life lasted a long time in Britain—over 350 years. During that time many people in Britain took to Roman ways—they learnt Latin, wore Roman clothes, obeyed Roman law, and so on. Only a few people in the Roman towns or villas were actually Romans. Most were British people who had become romanised—we call them Romano-British.

Romanisation was the way the Romans kept the peace in Britain after Boudica's revolt. The Roman writer Tacitus explained the point of this plan:

SOURCE 39

'The people used to be scattered and uncivilised and therefore ready for war. To make them peace-loving the Romans helped people to build squares, temples and houses. The sons of British leaders were trained in the Roman way of life . . . Roman clothes came into fashion . . . And little by little the Celts came to like the Roman way of life with its baths and banquets.' (Adapted.)

1 Explain what the Romans did to 'romanise' the British.
2 Explain how this policy made Roman Britain a peaceful land.

It is difficult to tell what the Romans were like, but we can certainly imagine them using the things in Sources 31–34. Some of the most moving things we find are tombstones, with inscriptions:

SOURCE 40

'To the memory of Simplicia Florentina, a most innocent soul. She lived 10 months. Her father, Felicius Simplex, soldier of the 6th Legion, set this up.'

'Julia Materna, aged six. Julius Marcellinus set this up for his beloved daughter.'

'Here lies Julius Valens, of the 2nd Legion. He lived 100 years. His wife Julia Secundina and son Julius Martinus had this made.'

1 What do these inscriptions tell us about the ages of the people who died in Roman times?
2 What do these inscriptions tell us about the feelings Roman families had for each other?

Source 6 showed us that the Roman Empire was an international Empire. People might work and live anywhere inside it, and meet people of many races. Source 41 tells such a story. It was found on Tyneside, and the inscription tells us that it was put up by a man named Barates, an ex-soldier from Palmyra, far away in Syria. At some point in his army career he bought Regina, a British slave, in East Anglia. Later he gave her her freedom and married her. The tombstone shows Regina with some of her belongings. Underneath the Latin, Barates has added, in his strange Palmyran writing, 'Regina, freed woman of Barates. Alas for her death!'

SOURCE 41 Tombstone from Tyneside

ASSESSMENT

Chronology

1 The successful Roman invasion of Britain took place in 43 AD. The Roman legions left Britain in 410 AD.
   a How many years were the Roman legions in Brtain for?
   b What year is it now? Take away the number of years from your answer to *a* from this year. What year do you get?
   c The second visit of Julius Caesar to Britain was in 54 BC. How many years was it from then until the successful invasion of 43 AD?
   d In what century did the Romans conquer Britain?
   e In what century did they leave Britain?

Similarity/ Difference

2 a Did the Romans have better living conditions than the Celts? In what ways?
   b The Romans called the Celtic people 'barbarians'. This means people who are totally uncivilised. Do you think the Celts were totally uncivilised? Do you think they were, in any way, more civilised than the Romans?
   c Would you rather live in a Roman house or your own home? Give reasons for your answer.

Making use of Evidence

SOURCE 42 Lead water-pipe

3 In what ways does this source provide us with evidence about:
   a Roman lettering?
   b Roman metalwork?
   c Roman hygiene?
   d Roman engineering?

ANGLO-SAXONS:

SOURCE 1 Anglo-Saxon hut

LOOK AT SOURCE 1 and compare it with Source 37 in Unit 1 (page 19). What a difference! The Roman villa at Lullingstone had many rooms, some of them very grand. There were mosaic floors, a bath-house and a central-heating system. Anglo-Saxon huts had none of these luxuries.

Yet Source 1 comes *later* in history than Source 37 —300 years later. You have just learnt something important about history and civilisation. Things do not always get better and better, like an escalator going ever upwards. Sometimes civilisation takes a step backwards.

Answer these questions in pairs.

1 What words would you use to describe the hut in Source 1?
2 What words would you use to describe the buckle (Source 2) and the Lindisfarne Gospels (Source 3)?
3 Using the evidence on these pages, do you think the Anglo-Saxons were: a) skilled? b) civilised?

Settlement and Church

Both the buckle in Source 2 and the Lindisfarne Gospels in Source 3 were made by Anglo-Saxon craftspeople.

SOURCE 2 Gold buckle made for an Anglo-Saxon leader

SOURCE 3 Page from Lindisfarne Gospels

AIMS

In this unit you will be finding out about the Anglo-Saxons. You will see why they are one of the most important of the many groups which go to make up the British people.

You will find out why they came to Britain, and how they settled here and eventually became the rulers of the country. You will also learn about the beginnings of CHRISTIANITY in Britain.

One of the difficulties of this early period of history for a historian is the shortage of written records from this time. We shall be looking at some of the written sources which do exist and seeing what problems there are in using them.

As we saw in Unit 1, historians also use archaeology to find out about the past. Archaeology is especially useful when there are hardly any written records. There are problems with archaeological sources, too, though, as we shall see.

Where did they come from?

TRIBES of Angles, Saxons and Jutes lived in Northern Europe, in what is now Denmark, Germany and the Netherlands (Source 4). These tribes were not Christians, but worshipped their own gods. They lived just outside the boundaries of the Roman Empire, and traded with the Romans. They sold objects made of leather, cloth and iron. The most precious thing they supplied was amber (a glowing yellow 'stone' which comes from fossilised resin). They were always looking for a chance to move into the richer areas controlled by the Romans. Only the Roman army kept them out.

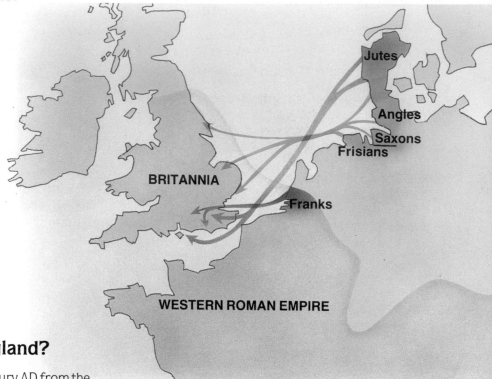

Why did they come to England?

Rome was under attack in the 4th century AD from the Goths, the Vandals and the Huns. The Angles, Saxons and Jutes were attacked too, so they wanted to move west to get away. As the Romans pulled their armies back to protect Rome, far-away parts of their Empire, such as Britain, had to be abandoned. This gave the Angles, Saxons and Jutes their chance. To them Britain seemed a rich and easy prize. There were precious objects and gold in the villas and towns. The fields were fertile. There were no high mountains to cross. The many rivers gave easy routes inland. Pushed by the Goths, Vandals and Huns the Angles, Saxons and Jutes began to raid the coasts of England. The Romano-British asked Rome for help in 410 AD. The reply came back: 'Look to your own defences'.

This was what the Romano-British tried to do. Short of soldiers, they decided to hire some tribes of Anglo-Saxons to fight off the others. In 428 the Anglo-Saxon chiefs, Hengist and Horsa, arrived with three shiploads of MERCENARIES. Once in England, the mercenaries and their Anglo-Saxon chiefs refused to go home. Sometime in the 440s (we don't know exactly when), they demanded more money, and then attacked the Romano—British.

It was at this point that the Anglo-Saxons began to take over and settle in England. This process took a long time.

SOURCE 4 This is where the Anglo-Saxons came from.

Was the Anglo-Saxon settlement violent?

SOURCE 5

'Swords glinted all around . . . In the middle of towns . . . bits of corpses . . . covered . . . with a purple crust of dried up blood . . . A number of wretched survivors were caught and butchered . . . others made for land beyond seas . . .'

Concerning the Ruin of Britain, by Gildas, a Romano-British monk, who died about 572 AD.

1 Gildas lived at the time of the events he was writing about. We can call his account a PRIMARY SOURCE OF EVIDENCE about the Anglo-Saxon invasions. Do you think his evidence is bound to be completely truthful?
2 What impression of the Anglo-Saxon settlement does Gildas give?
3 Gildas was a Christian monk. How would he feel about the Anglo-Saxons?
4 How might his feelings affect the story he told?

SOURCE 6

'These heathen conquerors devastated the cities and countryside . . . Public and private buildings were burnt; priests killed at the altar; bishops and people were destroyed with fire and sword and none remained to bury those who had suffered a cruel death.'

Bede's *History of the English Church and People*, written about 730 AD.

1 Look at the date: how close did Bede live to the events he was describing?
2 Bede wrote his account by reading what other people had written about the Anglo-Saxon invasions at the time. We call this a SECONDARY SOURCE OF EVIDENCE about the Anglo-Saxon invasions. What would you want to know before deciding whether Bede's is a truthful account of events in the 5th century?
3 What impression of the Anglo-Saxons does Bede give?
4 Which types of people does Bede seem most worried about?
5 What does this tell us about Bede?
6 Do we have enough reliable evidence, so far, to tell us the truth about the Anglo-Saxon settlement?
7 What other types of evidence would you like to have?

The trouble with finding out about the 5th and 6th centuries AD is that there are very few written records. The Anglo-Saxons were mostly illiterate, so left us nothing in writing. The Roman civilisation in Britain was disappearing, so written evidence from their side gets less and less.

When there are so few written sources, historians turn to archaeology, to see if objects can tell them anything.

The first thing we learn from archaeological evidence is that there were Anglo-Saxons in Britain before the Roman armies left. They were mostly soldiers in the Roman army, who settled in Britain when they retired.

The next thing the archaeologists can tell us is that there are very few signs of fire and destruction of Roman towns and villas. Most of these fell down through neglect and decay, rather than Anglo-Saxon violence. In many cases the Anglo-Saxons built their huts in the open spaces of Roman towns. They lived alongside Roman villas. There are even mixed cemeteries, where Christian Romans and pagan Anglo-Saxons are buried side by side. If they were prepared to die together they must have been prepared to live together.

1 What might Anglo-Saxons and Romans have had in common? What would have been the differences?
2 What do you think the Anglo Saxons thought of the Roman towns they were living in?
3 What would the Romano-British have thought of the Anglo-Saxon settlers?

There is evidence that the Romano-British did their best to keep their Roman way of life going, despite being cut off from Rome. St Germanus, a bishop in France, visited Britain in 429 and 447 and was met peacefully by Christian Romano-British leaders. The Roman town of Wroxeter, near Shrewsbury, was rebuilt on a large-scale sometime in the early 5th century.

However, the Roman way of life depended on an army, slaves, servants and contact with Rome. None of these things existed anymore. Gradually the villas, with their complicated heating systems, were abandoned. The big Roman town buildings were not maintained, and began to fall down. Of course, there were some battles as the Anglo-Saxons tried to push further westward, and the Romano-British leaders tried to stop them. But the Anglo-Saxons generally came in small family or tribal groups, of about 50–200 people, looking for places to live. They came to settle the land, not destroy it.

SOURCE 7

Anglo-Saxon style belt buckle, late 4th century, found in the Roman city of Colchester

Several more buckles, and some Anglo-Saxon style pottery have also been found, dating back to Roman times. How does this conflict with the impression of the Anglo-Saxon invasion given in Sources 5 and 6?

By the early 7th century Britain was divided up in the ways shown in Source 8. You can see from Source 8 that there were Romano-British still living in the West Country, Wales, Scotland and Ireland. In fact, the Anglo-Saxons never took over these areas. As we have seen, they came originally in small groups. By the early 7th century (200 years after Hengist and Horsa came) these small groups had begun to join up. Several little kingdoms were formed and these can be seen on the map.

Why are the Anglo-Saxons important?

The names of the kingdoms give you the first clue about why the Anglo-Saxons are important. Look at the names of some of these kingdoms: the Kingdom of the East Saxons, the Kingdom of the South Saxons, the Kingdom of the East Angles, the Kingdom of Kent. Essex, Sussex, East Anglia, and Kent are names we use today.

Quite soon after they arrived here the Anglo-Saxons began to call themselves the 'Englisc'. They called their new homeland 'Engle-land'. The English language of today comes from the language they spoke. There had been many settlers in Britain before the Anglo-Saxons came. After them have come other settlers, all of whom have added something to life in this country. But when we speak English, it is Anglo-Saxon words that we use.

Key
Celtic areas
- - - Approximate territorial boundaries

SOURCE 8 Britain in the early 7th century

Northumbria

Mercia

East Angles

East Saxons

West Saxons

South Saxons

Kent

ACTIVITY

Many village and town names come from the Anglo-Saxon. (A few are Viking or come from other languages.) The ending of the name is the clue:

-ton = village   *-ham* = farm   *-stead* = large farm   *-ing* = followers of   *-stock,* or *-stoke* = cattle farm
-ly, or *-ley,* or *-leigh* = clearing among woods or heath   *-field* = farmland surrounded by woods or heath

Mucking, therefore, means 'the place where the followers of Mucca (a Saxon chief) lived'. Ashton means 'a village by ash trees'. Sometimes two endings go together, like -ingham, meaning 'the farm of the followers . . .'

Working in pairs, look carefully at the map. Pick out all the places that have the endings above. Then draw a rough sketch map of the area, marking in all the places you've picked out, but giving their Anglo-Saxon meanings, e.g. Ardingly would be marked 'Clearing of the followers of Ard' on your map. If you have time, try to do the same thing for your own local area.

SOURCE 9 Map of part of Sussex

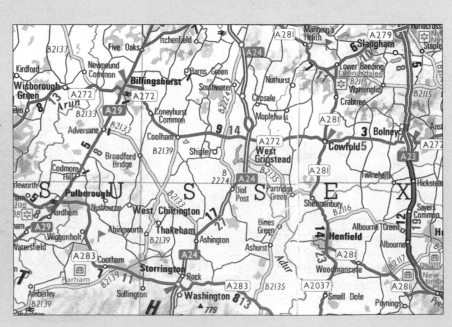

WHAT WERE THE ANGLO-SAXONS LIKE?

We shall try and use archaeology to answer this question as there are so few written documents from early Anglo-Saxon times. But there are problems with trying to learn from things we find in the ground.

> **Which of the following things, if buried in the ground, would *not* rot away after a thousand years:**
>
> **gold, wood, leather, human flesh, human bones, cloth, glass, iron, silver, paper?**

The Anglo-Saxons were skilled in using wood, leather and cloth, but very few of these materials survive. The fact that some of these things rot away makes it difficult for archaeologists to work out exactly what they have found. The two items below, Source 10 and Source 11, are two attempts to reconstruct a musical instrument to show what it might have looked like. Only the metal parts were found; all the wooden parts had rotted away.

> **1 Draw the metal parts which the archaeologists found. On the basis of these remaining parts, which reconstruction do you think is likely to be accurate? Explain your answer.**

2 Working in pairs, take Sources 12–17, one by one, and write a sentence on each saying what it tells us about the Anglo-Saxons. Compare your conclusions with other pairs. Then put together a class findings sheet called 'The Anglo-Saxons from their own evidence'.

SOURCE 12 Sword, with jewelled gold handle

SOURCE 13 Helmet, a reconstruction

SOURCE 10

SOURCE 11

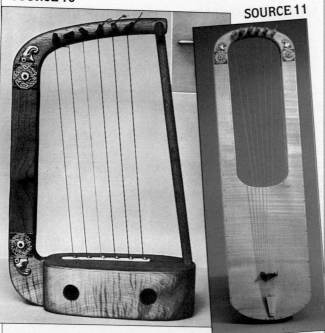

SOURCE 14 Shoulder clasp, gold with jewels

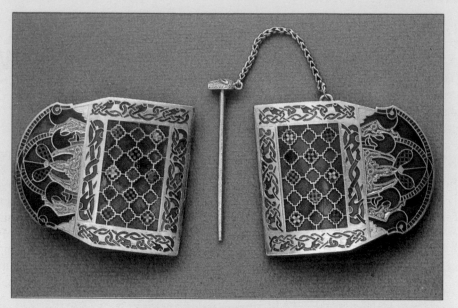

SOURCE 15 Bowl, made in Egypt, found in the same Anglo-Saxon grave as in Sources 10, 11, 12, 13 and 14

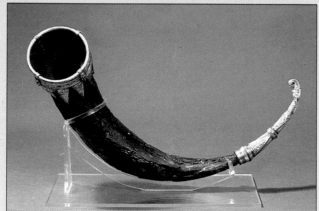

SOURCE 16 Drinking horn

SOURCE 17 From *Beowulf,* a long Anglo-Saxon poem of which we have 3182 lines. It tells the story of a great Anglo-Saxon warrior. Beowulf, the warrior, kills Grendel an evil sea-monster. King Hrothgar holds a feast to welcome him home.

'Hrothgar gave Beowulf an embroidered banner of gold, a helmet and a mail-coat . . .' The helmet had 'round the top . . . a projecting rim . . .' 'Songs were sung . . . to the accompaniment of music. The harp was struck, and many ballads recited . . . Laughter rang out; cupbearers poured wine from wonderfully made flagons (jugs).'

At the end of the feast 'Benches were cleared away, and pillows and bedding spread upon the floor'.

How did they live?

By taking these objects and studying them we may not be getting a true picture of Anglo-Saxon life. As we have seen, things made of wood, leather and cloth have rotted away. Also the objects in Sources 10–15 come from a huge burial at Sutton Hoo, in Suffolk. This was probably where the Anglo-Saxon king of East Anglia was buried. His life would hardly have been typical of life for the average family at that time.

When archaeologists EXCAVATED Anglo-Saxon villages they found several pits, and postholes, arranged as in Source 18. At first they reconstructed them as in Source 19. But a different reconstruction gives quite a different hut, as shown in Source 20.

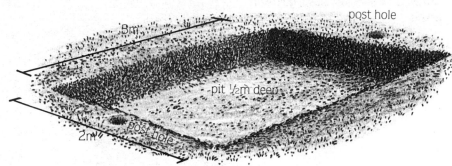

SOURCE 18 What the archaeologists found

SOURCE 19
First idea for the reconstruction using the pit

larger post giving a taller hut

SOURCE 20
The archaeologists' later reconstruction. The space under the floor planks was probably used for storage. This hut was drier and more comfortable

planks over the pit

SOURCE 21   Artist's reconstruction of the palace of King Athelstan at Cheddar, Somerset.

1   **Suggest three reasons why Source 21 may not be much help in deciding how a typical Anglo-Saxon family of the 7th century lived.**

2   **Imagine you are the chief steward to an Anglo-Saxon king (the person who makes all the arrangements for big feasts and banquets). Use Sources 10–17 to describe the preparations for a feast in the hall. Go on to describe what happened at the feast and what you saw of it from your position just behind the King's chair. Read out your description to a partner.**

Recently, archaeological evidence has been found in several places, of long, large buildings, perhaps 25 metres by 5 metres. These may have been halls, like Hrothgar's hall, where Beowulf was entertained. (See Source 17.)

We know much more about Anglo-Saxon kings than about ordinary people. We also know more about men than women, for much of our evidence comes from sources which are concerned only with the deeds of male warriors and rulers.

Kings were expected to be brave in war, wise and generous in peace, like King Hrothgar in Source 17. They also settled any arguments or disputes that arose in their lands. In this they were advised by their warriors and older men, the thanes.

For ordinary men, women and children the family was very important, and included all blood relations. People were expected to stick by their family at all times. Even law and order was based around the family. Arguments between families could lead to a blood-feud: if one member of a family was robbed or injured by a member of another family, revenge might be taken on any member of that family.

Anglo-Saxon women must have been important in holding the family together. Married women were expected to give way to their husbands, but single women had their own rights. In general, women were better off than before—in Roman times, or afterwards—in Norman times.

1   **In Unit 1 (page 21), you were asked to think about civilisation and to compare Romans and Celts. This time, make your comparison between the Romans and the Anglo-Saxons. Work in pairs, discussing the two civilisations. Some of the things to think about are: craft skills, art, homes, law, government.**
   Try to answer the question: who were the more civilised—Romans, or Anglo-Saxons?
   Are there any examples of Romans or Anglo-Saxons being more civilised than we are today?

BRITAIN BECOMES A CHRISTIAN COUNTRY

The Christian religion came to Britain in the 1st century AD. It was brought here by Roman Christians. At first these Christians were persecuted under the Romans. In Rome and elsewhere many Christians were killed. In 313, however, they were allowed to worship freely and in 393 Christianity became the official religion of the Roman Empire. It is likely that most of the Romano-British who faced the Anglo-Saxon invasions of the 5th century were Christians. After about 450, though, there is no evidence of Christianity in Britain.

The Anglo-Saxons were PAGANS. They worshipped their own family of gods: Woden, the king of the gods; Frig, the goddess of fertility; Tiw, the god of war and Thor, the god of thunder and the sky.

> **Which days of the week are named after these Anglo-Saxon gods?**

SOURCE 22 Bronze helmet showing an Anglo-Saxon god

They had other gods and goddesses too, such as Eostre, the moon goddess. She has given her name to the Christian festival of Easter.

The Anglo-Saxons arriving in England soon came across the Christian religion. We can perhaps tell something about their attitude to the Romano-British from their attitude to Christianity. At first they had little to do with it. Their gods were the gods of their family, and their tribe, and always had been. They could understand Woden, a great king among gods, just like their own chiefs. They found it difficult to understand the Christian God of peace, and poverty.

But the Christians taught about one God, and the Christian God was worshipped all over Europe. Which religion ought they to choose? Which would bring them success? Which would look after them in times of trouble? And what happened when you died? Many Anglo-Saxon chiefs and kings were very uncertain about these things.

The Roman Missionaries

Despite the raids from Goths, Vandals and Huns, Christianity survived in Rome. The head of the Church in Rome was called the Pope. In 590 AD, in Rome, Gregory I was elected Pope. There is a story that he once saw some Angles for sale as slaves in a Roman slave-market. 'They are not Angles but angels', he remarked, and decided to send missionaries to England. More likely, he was keen to increase the power of the popes. He thought he could do this by bringing England back into the Christian world.

In 597 Pope Gregory sent Augustine to England, to convert the Anglo-Saxons. Augustine went first to Kent. He arrived wearing his best robes, with his followers chanting and singing, and carrying bibles. He was welcomed by King Aethelberht, who had a Christian wife, Bertha. Churches were built at Canterbury and Rochester, and eventually King Aethelberht became a Christian. When Augustine and Aethelberht died in 605, however, Christianity disappeared from Kent.

SOURCE 23 Picture of Pope Gregory, from a book of about 740

Then, in 625, King Edwin of Northumbria married King Aethelberht's daughter. She took with her, on her journey northward, a Christian priest called Paulinus. King Edwin listened hard to Paulinus, but was unsure what to do. In 627 he called a meeting of all his advisers to discuss the new religion. One of King Edwin's chief men said:

SOURCE 24

'Your Majesty, when we compare our life on earth with the time before and after life, about which we know nothing, it seems to me like a flight of a sparrow through the banqueting hall. You are sitting at dinner on a winter's day, with all your thanes. In the middle is a comforting fire to warm the hall. Outside, the storms of winter rain or snow are raging. The sparrow flies quickly through one door of the hall and out of the other. While it is inside it is safe from the winter storms. But after a few moments of warmth it vanishes into the wintry world from whence it came.

So we appear on earth for a little while, but of what went before this life, or of what follows, we know nothing. If this new teaching has brought any more certain knowledge, it seems only right that we should follow it.'

Bede (adapted)

Then Coifi, the High Priest of the old religion, said he thought Paulinus brought 'Truths that will give us the blessings of life, salvation and eternal happiness'.

King Edwin took their advice and was converted to Christianity. Among the first to follow him was Coifi:

SOURCE 25

'Wearing a sword, and with a spear in his hand, Coifi mounted the King's stallion and rode to the statues of the old gods . . . When the crowd saw him they thought he had gone mad . . . but without any hesitation he threw his spear into the temple, and thus profaned it . . . (treated it with no respect). He then ordered his companions to set fire to the temples and destroy them all.

Bede (adapted)

1 **What do you think were the motives of the following people in becoming Christians: King Aethelberht? the speaker in Source 24? Coifi? King Edwin?**
2 **How do you think the ordinary people reacted to the decisions made by the King to change their religion?**
3 **What part did women play in the conversion of Kent and Northumbria to Christianity?**

Celtic Christianity in Northumbria

If you look at Source 8 you will see that the Romano-British were driven by the Anglo-Saxons into Western Britain and Ireland. Here the Christian religion survived, especially among the Celtic people of Ireland. They were, however, cut off from Rome, and developed their own customs.

In 563 St Columba had sailed across from Ireland and set up a small monastery on the island of Iona (Source 26). After King Edwin was killed in battle in 632, Christianity died down in Northumbria for a few years. But in 635, Oswald, Edwin's nephew, became king. He was a Christian. He had been to stay on the island of Iona. He invited some of the Iona monks to set up a monastery in his kingdom. Led by St Aidan, they built their monastery on Lindisfarne. This was an island at high tide, just opposite the castle of the Kings of Northumbria at Bamburgh.

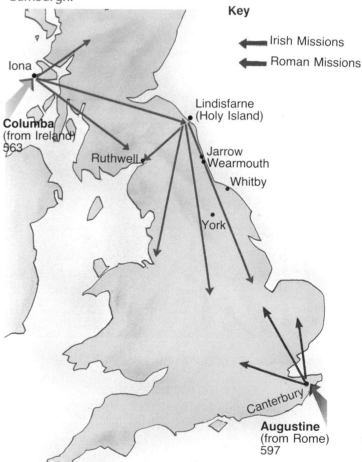

Key
← Irish Missions
← Roman Missions

Iona
Columba (from Ireland) 563
Lindisfarne (Holy Island)
Ruthwell
Jarrow
Wearmouth
Whitby
York
Canterbury
Augustine (from Rome) 597

SOURCE 26 Christian missionaries aimed to convert England from two directions.

Lindisfarne became the centre of a flourishing Christian community. From there, monks went out preaching and converting people all over Northumbria. At that time Northumbria was the most important kingdom in Britain,

SOURCE 27 St Peter's Church, Bradwell, Essex

and Lindisfarne began to send missionaries to the other kingdoms. Two brothers, St Cedd and St Chad, converted the people of Mercia. Later St Cedd became the BISHOP of the East Saxons. He built the church in Source 27, in about 660 AD. It is still standing today.

The most famous of the Lindisfarne SAINTS is St Cuthbert. He was born in 634 and became a monk at the age of 17. Many stories were told about him. When he was given the job of looking after guests at Ripon Abbey, he welcomed a young visitor one cold, wintry morning. He brought the visitor warm water, and hurried off to get some food. When he returned the young man had vanished, and there were no footprints in the fresh snow. Instead there was a wonderful smell of new-baked bread, and three fresh loaves on the table. Cuthbert was sure his visitor was an angel.

He became PRIOR (the most important monk) at Lindisfarne in 664. From there he travelled all over northern England and southern Scotland (which at this time was all part of the great kingdom of Northumbria). He made a point of visiting the wildest and loneliest farms and villages that no other preacher would go to.

He liked best being alone, with time to pray and think about God. In 676 he retired to Farne Island, an uninhabited island a few miles from Lindisfarne. Here he built himself a round cell, with high walls. He also made friends with many of the wild creatures that visited Farne Island. Sea-otters were said to dry his feet with their fur after he had been in the sea to wash. The eider ducks were his favourite animals, and were nick-named 'St Cuthbert's chickens'.

SOURCE 28 A 12th century picture of St Cuthbert and the sea-otters

He died in 687 and was buried at Lindisfarne. After his death many people visited his tomb. They hoped St Cuthbert, who they believed was in heaven, would make sure God heard their prayers.

1 What sort of man do you think St Cuthbert was?
2 How would the stories told about him help to spread the Christian religion among Anglo-Saxons?
3 Why do you think people are less ready to believe stories like these today?

In 689, St Cuthbert's tomb was opened. In honour of this great event, Eadfrith, a monk at Lindisfarne, designed, painted and wrote a copy of the gospels. The opening page of each gospel has a huge letter, elaborately decorated, which takes up most of the page. Source 29 shows the beginning of St Matthew's Gospel. There are also five 'carpet' pages, which are just patterns, with no letters, like Source 3. Eadfrith used 45 different coloured inks, all made from natural objects, such as oak apples, insects, flowers, fruit and ground-up stones. He marked out his page using rulers, compasses and pin-pricks. In spite of the complicated designs there were no mistakes.

The Power of the Church

Source 26 (page 32) shows how England was converted from two directions: Roman missionaries from Canterbury, and Celtic missionaries from Iona and Lindisfarne. This caused problems, as there were small, but important differences between them.

For instance, they held their Easter celebrations on different dates. In the household of King Oswy of Northumbria this was very awkward, as he followed the Celtic date, and his wife the Roman.

He therefore called a big church meeting—a SYNOD—at Whitby in 664 to decide between the two systems. Wilfred, Abbot of Ripon, the spokesman for the Roman system, won the argument.

From then on Roman rules, customs and services began to be used all over Britain. For almost 870 years after the Synod, the Pope was the head of the Christian church in England.

Northumbria continued to be a centre of learning in the 7th and 8th centuries. Benedict Biscop, Abbot of Wearmouth, expanded the monastery there in the 680s. He had it re-built in stone, and founded another abbey nearby, at Jarrow. Craftsmen put stained glass in the windows, and Biscop brought books from all over Europe. Soon he had the best library outside Rome.

Bede, whose writings you have already come across, lived in Jarrow. He was born in 672 and went into Wearmouth monastery at the age of seven. A few years later he moved to Jarrow where he spent the rest of his

SOURCE 29 Initial letter of Lindisfarne Gospel—St Matthew

life. He taught people who came to him at Jarrow, and worked on his great *History of the English Church and People*. He tried hard to find out everything he could about the coming of the Anglo-Saxons and their conversion to Christianity. He also tried to separate facts from stories, and truth from opinions.

1 Bede wrote his *History* without moving from Jarrow. How do you think he did this? What sources could he have used?
2 Do you think his writings are less reliable than primary sources because he did not himself live at or near the time of the events he wrote about?
3 Do you think historians should put their own opinions into their books?
4 Do you think it is possible to avoid putting your own opinions into what you write?
5 Do you think history teachers should tell their pupils their opinion of things?

In 669, after the Synod of Whitby, the Pope appointed Theodore of Tarsus to be Archbishop of Canterbury. Theodore was from Greece, but set about organising the CHURCH in this new land of England, far from home. He divided England up into areas, called DIOCESES. Most were about the size of a county, although some, like the diocese of Lincoln, were much bigger. Each diocese was run by a bishop. Each bishop was based in a large church, called a cathedral. Every diocese was divided up into PARISHES. A parish was usually made up of one village. Most of the parish boundaries of England date from this time. Eventually, every parish was to have its own church, and its own PRIEST. For this, Theodore set up schools to educate people to become priests.

It was a long time before there was a church in every parish—two or three centuries. Until the village could get enough money to build a church, the Anglo-Saxons put up preaching-crosses. Priests would hold the service in the open air by the cross.

During the next few centuries, the bishops and priests worked to convert the Anglo-Saxons (and later, the Vikings) to Christianity. The church played a very important part in the life of each parish. It was not only the place where people were BAPTISED, married and buried. It was also the place where the village met, to hear what the government wanted to tell them. It was the only place where they could all meet for feasts and other gatherings. The priest often ran the only schools that there were. The church was used to store items like fire-fighting buckets and ladders. The church bells were the village alarm signal.

The system of dioceses and parishes set up by Theodore of Tarsus has lasted until the present day, with a few alterations. In Anglo-Saxon times it meant that the Church had an organisation that covered the whole country. Until the 10th century there were still several separate kingdoms, so the Church was important in uniting England. With priests, and a strong organisation, the Church was to be central to the life of England for the next thousand years.

1 Divide your page into nine small boxes: In the middle box, draw a cross, like the one at Ruthwell. In each of the other eight boxes, draw a picture to illustrate the importance of the Church in the life of a parish.
2 Make a list of all the ways that the Church made Anglo-Saxon England a more civilised country.

SOURCE 30
The Ruthwell Cross is an example of a preaching cross found in villages without a church. It is 6 metres high, with carvings of Christ on the front, and carving down the sides.

ASSESSMENT

Primary and Secondary Sources

SOURCE 31

'The men went to Catterick, raising the war-cry, javelins aloft and sharp lances, bright armour and swords.
    The men went to Catterick, they were famous. Wine and mead from gold cups was their drink. Of all that hurried out after that drink, none escaped but three.
    The men went to Catterick, swift was their army. Three hundred battling according to plan and after the glad war-cry there was silence.'

From a poem written in about 600 AD. It describes a battle fought near Catterick, Yorkshire.

SOURCE 32

'It was mainly the wealthier Saxons who owned swords. At first the swords had wooden, or bone handles, but later some of them were decorated with gilt, silver and jewels. Swords were treasured weapons and many were handed down from father to son. Some Saxons wore armour, but not all of them wore helmets. They fought on foot, although they often rode to battle on horseback.'

From a book about the Saxons written by Ray Mitchell and Geoffrey Middleton in 1979.

1 a Look at sources 31 and 32. Which is a primary source about warfare in Anglo-Saxon times?
  b Which is a secondary source about warfare in Anglo-Saxon times?
  c How can you tell?
  d Why do you think the poem, Source 31, was written?
  e Suggest reasons why Source 32 may not be a completely reliable source of evidence about Anglo-Saxon warfare.
  f How do you think the writers of Source 32 were able to find out about the things they have written about?
  g How far do Sources 31 and 32 agree with each other in their descriptions of Anglo-Saxon warfare?
  h What are the main differences?
  i Suggest reasons for these differences.

Making use of Evidence

SOURCE 33 Saxon necklace. It is made of gold with red garnets (precious stones) set in gold.

SOURCE 34

Saxon glass beaker. It has a rounded end so will not stand up. Saxons had to drain the beaker at one drink!

2 a What does Source 33 tell us about the lives of women in Anglo-Saxon times?
  b If several necklaces like this were found, would this make a difference to your answer to question 2a?
  c Does the necklace prove the wearer was a Christian?
  d What does Source 34 tell us about Anglo-Saxon life?
  e What do Sources 33 and 34 tell us about the craft skills of the Anglo-Saxons?

Chronology

3 Using the second part of this unit, draw up a time-line, marking in important dates and events to do with religion.
4 Give two reasons why it is important for people living today to know something about the Anglo-Saxons.

King Alfred ~ The Great?

SOURCE 1 Modern-day heroes and heroines.

DO YOU HAVE A HERO, or a heroine? Is his or her picture here? Who is the person most admired by everyone in your class?

History is full of heroes and heroines. One great hero of the British people is King Alfred. Many stories were told about Alfred. This is the most famous:

SOURCE 2
'One day, a certain woman, the wife of a cow-herd, was making bread, and Alfred the King was sitting by the fire mending his bow and arrows. When the poor woman saw that the loaves of bread were burning she ran up, saying, "Look there, man, you can see the loaves are burning and you've not turned them. I'm sure you'd be the first to eat them if they were properly cooked". This woman little thought that this was King Alfred who had fought so many wars and won so many victories.'

From the Annals of St Neots, early 12th century

1 This is the earliest record we have of the story of Alfred and the cakes. Historians look on the story as a LEGEND—a tale made up about a hero and possibly not true. Why do they think this?
2 Can we be certain that it is untrue?
3 If it is a legend, has it any value for a historian?

AIMS

In this unit we shall be finding out about King Alfred. We shall see how he dealt with the brave and fierce Viking invaders. We shall see how he built up his Anglo-Saxon kingdom of Wessex into a NATION-STATE. He became a hero to many people in his own lifetime. By the end of the unit you should be able to decide for yourself whether you think he was a hero. Is his greatness real or is it a MYTH?

SOURCE 3 Statue of Alfred in Wantage.

We are lucky to have some primary sources of evidence about Alfred. The main one is the *Life of Alfred* written by Bishop Asser. Asser was a Welsh monk who was Alfred's friend and helper. Alfred made him Bishop of Sherborne. Just because Asser's book is a primary source does not mean that it is totally reliable. It may be BIASED. Alfred was Asser's hero and so Asser may have tried to make him out to be greater than he really was. The story that follows is based on Asser's account. As you read it, try to think of ways in which it may be biased.

Alfred as a child

Alfred was born in 849, at Wantage. England at that time was still divided into several kingdoms. His father was Ethelwulf, Anglo-Saxon King of Wessex. His mother was called Osburh. It seemed unlikely that he would ever be King as he had three older brothers. In fact, his father probably wanted Alfred to become a priest: he was sent to visit the Pope, in Rome, twice, before he reached the age of nine.

SOURCE 4 Map of England at the time of Alfred

Strathclyde

Galloway

Northumbria

Gwynedd

Powys

MERCIA

East Anglia

Dyfed

Essex

WESSEX

Kent

Sussex

Asser tells an interesting story about Alfred's childhood. His mother promised a beautiful book of poems to whichever of her sons could learn the book by heart. Alfred, although the youngest, got someone to teach him the poems, and he won the prize.

> 1 If this story is true, what does it tell us about Alfred, and perhaps about his brothers?
> 2 If it is not true, but made up by Alfred or by Asser, what does it tell us about the kind of hero they wanted to create?

These were not peaceful times to grow up in.

The Vikings

England was being attacked at this time by the Vikings. Norway, Sweden and Denmark did not have much fertile land. Eldest sons could make a living on the little farms, and from fishing. Younger sons had to seek their fortune overseas. They joined up in groups of a few dozen, a few hundred or even a few thousand and raided other lands.

The Vikings were brave seamen. In open boats, like the one in Source 7, they sailed the North Sea and raided the coasts of Britain and France. They sailed the Atlantic to Iceland, Greenland and Labrador. They sailed into the Mediterranean, and up the great rivers into Russia and Europe. The boats could ride the waves of the North Atlantic but they were also shallow enough to go up small rivers into the heart of prosperous farmlands.

'Viking' means pirate, and the Vikings seized food, drink, horses, gold and whatever else they wanted. They worshipped their own gods and destroyed Christian churches and monasteries. They were very tough: they were able to survive for many days in an open boat at sea. The Vikings often had to row for hours, then fight with swords and axes. They believed that to die a 'cow's death' at home in bed sent you to hell. If you died fighting you went to feast for ever in Valhalla, the hall of Odin, king of the gods. They took no prisoners and left the wounded to die. If they captured a king, he suffered the 'blood eagle'—his ribs and lungs were cut out and spread beside him like eagle's wings.

England—a rich, fertile country not far across the sea from Denmark—was an obvious target for Danish Viking raids. In 793 the great Northumbrian abbey of Lindisfarne (see Unit 2 page 32) was attacked and burnt. Raids took place almost every year after that.

Soon after Alfred was born, things became more serious. In 850—1, instead of going home after their summer raid, the Danes spent the winter on the Isle of Thanet in Kent. They began to look for places to settle permanently. In 866 York was burnt down and Northumbria was taken over by the Danes. In 869 Edmund, King of East Anglia, was defeated and suffered the 'blood eagle'. The Vikings then turned their attention to Wessex.

SOURCE 7 Viking ship found at Oseberg in Norway

SOURCE 5 Carving from Oseberg ship

SOURCE 6 Carving from ship found in Netherlands

SOURCE 8 Map of Viking invasions

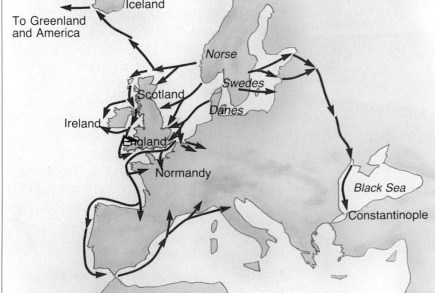

To Greenland and America — Iceland — Norse — Swedes — Scotland — Danes — Ireland — England — Normandy — Black Sea — Constantinople

What evidence do these sources give us about the skills of the Vikings?

Alfred meets the Danes

By this time Alfred was a young man of 20. His mother had died when he was seven and his father when he was ten. Two of his brothers had also died. Alfred had learnt to hunt and to fight, like any other royal prince at that time.

Wessex had not suffered much while the Danes were busy in Northumbria and East Anglia. But in 870 they sailed up the Thames and made camp near Reading. The next year they marched from there into Wessex along the Ridgeway path. Alfred and his remaining brother, Ethelred, led the Wessex army and met the Danes near the White Horse at Uffington, on Ashdown.

While his brother was still praying for victory, Alfred led a fierce charge up the hill and defeated the Danes. The victory did not last long. Nine more battles were fought in that year, 871 AD, most of them won by the Danes. Alfred's brother died and Alfred became King of Wessex at the age of 22. As the difficult year of 871 drew to a close, he paid the Danes money to leave Wessex for a while.

For the next few years the Danes turned their attention to Mercia (see Source 4). Half the kingdom was taken and the King, Alfred's brother-in-law, fled. That left Wessex as the only surviving Anglo-Saxon kingdom. It would not be long before the Danes attacked again.

In 876, the Danish king, Guthrum, landed with an army at Wareham. Alfred met them and arranged a truce. The Danes then slipped away to Exeter, but Alfred again followed, and made peace. In 877 the Danish Army moved into Mercia and Alfred spent Christmas at Chippenham. Then Guthrum made a clever move: he knew that Alfred would not expect an attack in winter, and that the 'Twelfth Night' of Christmas was a time of great feasting. He knew there would be plenty of food at Chippenham for the festivities, which would keep his Danish army supplied. So on January 5th 878 Guthrum attacked Alfred at Chippenham and scattered his army.

Alfred was now at his lowest point. Wessex lay wide open to the Danes and many people fled abroad. Alfred had no army and retreated to Athelney in the Somerset Levels. In those days it was a marshy place of thickets and soggy reedbeds. Only local people, like Alfred, who had lived nearby knew the secret paths and waterways. Here he was safe and could organise his fight-back. It was here that he is supposed to have burnt the loaves.

SOURCE 9 Alfred meets the Danes at Uffington

SOURCE 10 Uffington White Horse

The Battle of Edington

At Whitsun, in 878, Alfred ordered all his followers to meet him. They rallied to him and he defeated the Danes at the Battle of Edington. This is how Asser describes the events:

SOURCE 11

'He attacked the whole pagan army, fighting ferociously in dense order, and by divine will eventually won the victory, made great slaughter among them and chased them to Chippenham. Everything left outside their camp, men, horses and cattle, he seized, killing the men. After 14 days, the pagans were brought to the extreme depths of despair by hunger, cold and fear and they sought peace.'

ACTIVITY

Now, in pairs, read the account that follows. It tells what happened after the battle. It is not written in the same style as Asser's writing. Together, rewrite it, trying to imitate Asser's style. Alfred must come out of it as the great Christian hero.
Read some of your accounts to the rest of the class. Decide whose works best and why.

When the Danes surrendered, Alfred took Guthrum and 30 of his most important men prisoners. He took them to Aller church, near Athelney, and made them become Christians. Alfred then entertained them for 12 days at his hall at Wedmore. They agreed to leave Wessex and never return. Alfred agreed to let them have all of East Anglia, Northumbria and Mercia to the North and East of Watling Street. This area was called the Danelaw. England was thus a land divided between two peoples.

THE DANES IN ENGLAND

Guthrum kept his word. His people settled throughout the Danelaw. Most of them were farmers, but the towns of York, Leicester, Nottingham, Derby, Lincoln and Stamford flourished. The Danes kept up their links with Denmark and traded in many things across the North Sea. They were also skilled at crafts of metal, wood, horn and stone.

Part of one of their towns, at York, has recently been excavated. The archaeological finds tell us a great deal about Viking York—or Jorvik as they called it.

SOURCE 12 20th century reconstruction of a loom in a Viking home at Jorvik

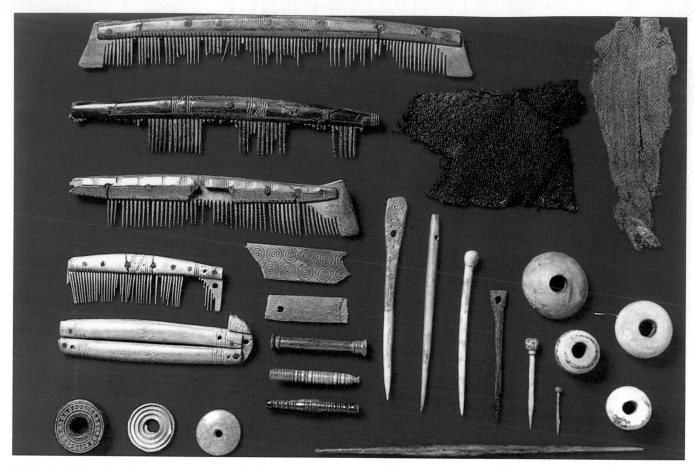

SOURCE 13 Combs, spinning weights and pins from Jorvik. These are made from horn and bone.

SOURCE 14 Large pot (½ metre high) used for storing wine, from Jorvik

SOURCE 15 Viking carvings on bone of the Jorvik period

1 Are Sources 12, 13, 14 and 15 primary or secondary sources of evidence about Jorvik?

2 What do Sources 12 and 14 tell us about the Viking way of life?

3 How do you think the historians and artists who made Source 13 got their information?

4 Which is the most useful source in helping us to understand life in Jorvik?

The Danish language lives on in place names ending in -thorpe, -toft or -by. Many dialect words remain in Yorkshire and Lincolnshire, such as this way of counting sheep up to ten, used until quite recently:

Yahn, Tayn, Tethera, Methera, Mump
Hithera, Lithera, Auver, Dauver, Dic.

Many ordinary words in English come from the Danish too: *take*; *call*; *husband*; *sky*; *window*; *anger*; *low*; *loose*; *ugly*; *wrong*; *happy*; *ill*; *die*; *bread*, and *eggs*, for example. In this way the Vikings made their contribution to the mixture of races and languages that go to make up the British people and the English language.

Although Guthrum promised to keep the peace made at Wedmore, Alfred was taking no chances. The Danes had been known to break their word. There were other Viking armies in Europe too—such as the one which beseiged Paris in 888. They might turn to attack Wessex. Alfred worked hard to organise his kingdom to meet this threat. He made military preparations. He also turned his attention to education. He wanted to supply his GOVERNMENT with well-educated people. He improved the system of JUSTICE in Wessex. In doing all these things, he became more like a king and less like an Anglo-Saxon chief.

The Defence of Wessex

The Army (the fyrd)

Apart from Alfred's personal bodyguard of a few dozen men, there was no regular army. Every man in Wessex was supposed to turn out and fight if called upon. Men were reluctant to stay in the army for more than a few weeks, though. They did not like neglecting their farms.

SOURCE 16 Burh at Cricklade, Wiltshire. The rectangle of the burh can still be seen, 1100 years later. The main street, side streets, lanes, houses and gardens run at right angles to each other. The ramparts can still be seen on the left. They are not very high now, but those at Wareham were still big enough to be used as anti-tank defences in 1940

Alfred needed an army to be on watch all the time. He therefore divided the fyrd into two halves: half the men could stay at home to look after the land, while the others were in the fyrd. They would then change over.

The Navy

The Danish attack on Wareham in 877 had shown Alfred the advantage of having good ships. He ordered his own ships to be built—longer and stronger than the Vikings' ships. Alfred's had 30 oars down each side.

The Burhs

Over the last 20 years of his life, Alfred planned and laid out 29 burhs, or royal towns. They were places of trade and business. They were also strong-points in case of attack. Some controlled rivers. Others were placed so that nowhere in Wessex was more than 20 miles from a burh. In times of danger people could take refuge behind their ramparts.

> 1 What can an aerial photograph of a town show that other pictures of the town can not?
> 2 What does the aerial photograph not show?

SOURCE 17 Street plan of Wareham

The people of Wessex were not keen to spend money and time on the burhs. When another Danish army attacked in 892 they were not ready. The Danes were, however, driven off by 896 and the growth of the burhs continued.

In 896 Alfred took London, which had belonged to Mercia. He laid out the streets between Cheapside and the River Thames in the 890s. Although there are towering office-blocks there today, the lines of the streets are still as Alfred laid them out.

Alfred and Education

Alfred lived 500 years before printing was invented. Books had to be written out by hand. This was usually done by monks, perhaps working in twos or threes, copying out the words from an original. This meant that books were very rare and precious. They were also easily destroyed—fire could consume six months' work in five minutes. The monasteries had been favourite targets for the Danes. Monks did not fight back, and the monasteries contained food, gold and precious objects. Many books were destroyed in Danish attacks.

Without books there could be no education. Alfred himself grew up unable to read and write. He later learnt these skills. Hardly any of the priests or the great men of Wessex could read and write either. At that time Latin was the language used by educated people for serious writing. It was the language of church services, and was used and understood throughout Europe. Alfred himself wrote about the standard of Latin in England:

SOURCE 19

The Alfred Jewel. This was found near Athelney. It is made of gold and crystal and says on it, in Anglo-Saxon, AELFRED MEC HEHT GEWYRCAN—Alfred had me made. It shows one of the five senses—sight. A long stick fitted in the hole at the bottom. The 'Jewel' then became the handle of a pointer, for following the place in a book.

1 **What does the 'Alfred Jewel' tell us about Alfred's feelings about skilled craft work?**
2 **What do both Source 18 and 19 tell us about Alfred's attitude to education, books and learning?**

SOURCE 18

'So general was its decay in England that there were very few south of the Humber who could understand church services in English or translate a letter from Latin into English. And I believe there were not many beyond the Humber. There were so few, I cannot remember a single one south of the Thames when I came to the throne.'

Some people think Alfred exaggerated how bad things were when he came to the throne. Why might he have done this?

Alfred realised that he needed well-educated servants in his government. First of all, he brought in educated people, usually priests, from Mercia. One of these was Asser. He taught Alfred to read and write Latin and Anglo-Saxon himself. Together they translated a few books which they thought were important, from Latin into Anglo-Saxon. These included Bede's *History of the English People* which you read about in Unit 2. There was also a book called *Pastoral Care*, which told bishops how to do their job. Alfred also had the story of the kings of Wessex written down, up to his own victory at Edington. This account was called the *Anglo-Saxon Chronicles* and several copies were made. One was sent to every monastery, and the monks had to keep it up to date by recording the main events of each year. Seven copies of the Anglo-Saxon Chronicles have been found, one of which was kept right up to the 12th century.

Alfred insisted that his officials, and earls should learn to read and write, if not in Latin, then in Anglo-Saxon. As Asser records, most of them did as they were told:

SOURCE 20

'Wonderful to say, almost all his earls and officers, though uneducated from their cradles, were bent on learning, preferring to work at this rather than lose their jobs. But if any one of them, from old age, or slowness, was unable to make progress he ordered his son, or a relative, or a servant to recite Saxon books to him, day and night. They sighed deeply in their inmost hearts that they had never studied in their youth. And they blessed the young men of our days who could learn . . .'

1 **Explain how each of the three books translated would have helped Alfred in his role as King.**
2 **Do you think Asser is telling us the whole story about what these adults felt when forced to go to school?**

The Laws

Imagine what would happen if school rules were not written down, or if no-one could read them! Pupils wouldn't know if they were breaking the rules or not. Different teachers might give out punishments for different things. Alfred realised that to be fair to his people his laws would have to be written down. There would have to be people who could read, too.

Justice had to be simple in Alfred's day—there were no prisons and no police force. He was also ruler of Wessex, Kent and part of Mercia, all of which had slightly different laws. Some Danes settled in his lands, too, and they had different laws. He therefore collected all the laws together and made one set for all his people.

The old Anglo-Saxon system of the blood-feud was replaced by the system of the 'wergild'. This gave the person injured by a crime the right to claim money, the 'wergild', as compensation. It was a lot less barbaric than the blood feud. Alfred fixed the wergilds to be paid, depending on the seriousness of the injury and the importance of the injured person. Breaking a person's little finger meant a 'wergild' of 1/- (5p); knocking out a back tooth was 4/- (20p). An injury to a 'thane' (noble) cost six times as much as an injury to a 'ceorl' (peasant). Alfred tried to enforce the Church's rules: the 'wergild' was £6 for breaking the rule about fasting in Lent.

The wergild to be paid if your dog savaged someone to death was only 6/- (30p) for the first offence. It was 12/- (60p) if the dog did it again, and 30/- (£1.50) if it claimed a third victim!

Disputes over land and property were resolved in an open court. Villagers who knew the situation well, gave their version of the truth. This old Anglo-Saxon custom is the beginning of our system of trial by jury. Someone accused of a crime could be given a trial by ordeal. There were four of these: Ordeal by Cake meant having to eat a cake which had been blessed by a priest. If you coughed or choked you were guilty. Ordeal by Cold Water meant being thrown into a pond, with a rope tied to you. If you were innocent you would sink, and the rope was used to haul you out. Ordeal by Hot Water meant picking a stone out of the bottom of a bucket of boiling water. Your hand was bound up and if it healed in three days you were innocent. Ordeal by Fire was similar—you had to hold a hot iron and walk three paces. Again, you were innocent if the burn had healed in three days.

Get into groups of three or four.

1 **Write down the good and bad points about Alfred's legal system.**
2 **Make up five different 'wergilds' to fit our 20th century way of life. Would you have different 'wergilds' for different people?**
3 **Why do you think we don't have wergilds and trials by ordeal nowadays?**

The system of trial by ordeal seems brutal to us today. We must remember though, that everyone at that time had a strong, simple religious belief. They were really asking God to decide. The Church also offered mercy to criminals. If you were running away from the law and went into a church you would be safe. The priests would encourage you to confess, if you were guilty, or help you to go abroad.

SOURCE 21 Sanctuary knocker, Durham Cathedral. If you held this knocker on the north door of Durham Cathedral you were safe from the law.

All over Western Europe the Vikings were successful in overthrowing kings and local rulers. Only in Wessex were they met by a King who drove them off. In doing this, Alfred saved the Anglo-Saxons from being completely overrun by the Vikings. He also made Wessex into a well-run kingdom. His grandsons, Aethelstan and Edgar, were the first kings of all England. The system of government Alfred set up in Wessex became the basis of royal rule in England from the 10th century onwards.

A thousand years after Alfred came to the throne, in 1871, Britain was a powerful country, with an Empire all over the world. (You will find out about this in Books 2 and 3.) People at that time looked back into the beginnings of British history to see where their greatness began. Alfred thus became a hero to the people of the 19th century. The statue (Source 3), was put up in 1871.

History books told a glorious tale:

SOURCE 22

'He was an example to princes, an ornament to human nature. To give a character of Alfred would only be to sum up those qualities which make up perfection. Even virtues which seem opposite were happily blended in his character: just yet merciful, determined yet ready to listen to others, stern in command yet gentle in conversation. Nature also had given him all physical gifts; vigour, dignity and an engaging, open face.'

Adapted from '*A History of England*' published in the 19th century

SOURCE 23 Illustration from child's history book

SOURCE 24 9th century coin showing the head of Alfred

Even when he was alive, Alfred was built up by Asser to be a hero. Many of the things Alfred wanted to do—building up his navy, his army and his towns—cost money, so it was important that the people should like him. People were more likely to pay their taxes willingly if they thought of their ruler as a great hero. We must be cautious about relying too much on Asser's word. We must use all the evidence to make up our own minds whether Alfred was indeed 'great'.

1 Look at Sources 22, 23 and 24. Which one do you think is likely to be the most accurate?
2 Why do you think the legend of Alfred and the burning of the cakes is such a popular story?
3 Why do you think legends start up about heroes and heroines? Why do you think legends are often more popular than the truth?

ASSESSMENT

Role of the Individual

Now is the time to make your own mind up about Alfred. It might be best to discuss your answers to 1 and 2 in a group before coming to a decision.

1 For each of the following turning points, decide:
   a what Alfred could have done;
   b what he did;
   c why he did this.

The turning points are:
   I Facing the Danes at Ashdown with his brother in 871.
   II Being driven out of his hall at Chippenham in January, 878.
   III Hiding at Athelney in the early months of 878.
   IV After the battle of Edington, Whitsun, 878.

2 Look over the whole unit. Is there anything we know for sure that Alfred did which you think counts *against* him? (Why are these incidents very important to us, given the kind of evidence we have?)

3 a Look back over the section, 'Alfred in Peace'. Pick out five or six important things which he did in order to rule and establish government.
   b Was Alfred a good ruler?

4 Putting together your answers to 1, 2 and 3, do you think Alfred deserves the title 'The Great'? Write a paragraph giving your conclusions.

5 Who else is 'great' in history? Do you have to be famous to be great? Do you have to be successful to be great? Do you have to be a king, or a ruler, to be great? Discuss these issues in groups of four and then report back your group decisions to the rest of the class.

THE NORMAN INVASION AND CONQUEST

WHEN EDWARD THE CONFESSOR died in 1065, it was not clear who should SUCCEED him to the throne. Some wanted to choose his nearest male blood-relation. He had no son, so the choice was not easy (Source 2). Others said the best man in the family should be chosen even if he wasn't the closest blood-relation.

SOURCE 1 Death of Edward the Confessor

SOURCE 2 *A simplified* family tree of Edward the Confessor

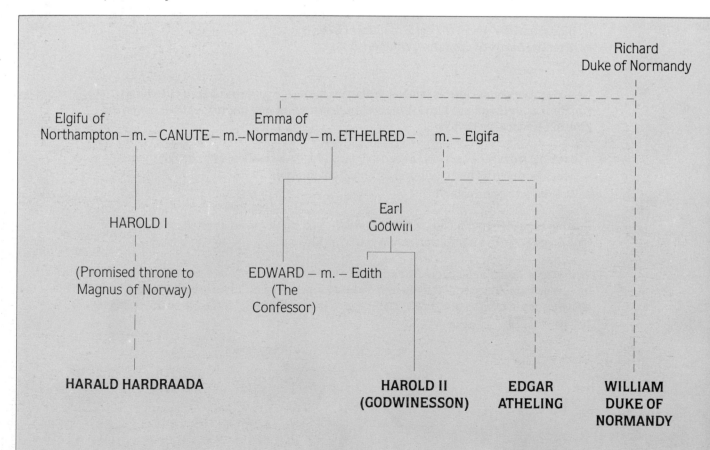

All the characters in Sources 3, 4, 5 and 6 believed they had a claim to the throne.

49

SOURCE 3 Harold Godwinesson

SOURCE 5 William Duke of Normandy

SOURCE 4 Harald Hardraada

SOURCE 6 Edgar 'The Atheling'

You are the members of the WITAN, the King's council, made up of leading English barons. You have the right to decide who will be king. In groups of 4 discuss the claims of each of the characters.

1 What qualities are you looking for in a king?
2 Who was the closest relation to Edward?
3 What questions would you want to ask those claiming the throne?

AIMS

In this unit you will be exploring the motives of the people who wanted to become King of England. You will see how different sources disagree about these motives. You will discover how the dispute over Edward's succession led to the Norman invasion of Britain.

The Normans not only invaded England, they also successfully conquered the country. The fact that they did so is very important in England's history. The Norman Conquest was the last successful conquest of England. It brought many changes to the country and led to much closer contact between England and the rest of Europe.

Use Source 2 to help you understand this section.

Claim 1: Edgar the 'Atheling'

Edward Atheling ('the Outlaw') was the son of King Edmund, who was Edward the Confessor's brother. When the Viking King Canute invaded Britain, Edward the Outlaw was sent far away to Hungary. He returned to England in 1057, hoping to become king after the Confessor's death. He died the same year, however, leaving a son, Edgar. When Edward the Confessor died, Edgar was only 14. The leading noblemen of England did not think he was a suitable claimant for the throne.

Claim 2: Harold Godwinesson

1 Harold was Edward the Confessor's brother-in-law. Edward's marriage to Edith is written about in the *Anglo-Saxon Chronicles*. We have here several different sources of evidence. Three main texts have survived, written by monks at Abingdon, Worcester and Peterborough between 1050 and 1150. To compile their chronicles, the monks used documents dating back to the late 800s.

SOURCE 8 Edward's marriage to Edith, Harold's sister, in 1045

SOURCE 7 Page from the *Anglo-Saxon Chronicles*

2 In 1066 Harold was the most powerful man in England. He ruled Wessex, which covered most of Southern England. He was related to most of the other leading earls. Also he had already proved himself in battle:

SOURCE 9

'Earl Harold and his brother, Earl Tostig, went into Wales with both a land force and a naval force and subdued the country.'

Anglo-Saxon Chronicles, 1063.

---

3 Harold was present at Edward's death.

SOURCE 10

'Stretching forth his hand to Harold, he (Edward) said "I commend this woman (Edith) and all the kingdom to your protection".'

This text comes from *The Life of King Edward*. It was probably written by a monk shortly after the King's death. It was dedicated to Edith, Edward's wife.

Source 11 comes from the Bayeux Tapestry. This is an embroidery in coloured wools, 70 metres long and half a metre wide. It was made shortly after the Norman Conquest by English nuns at Canterbury. It was made for the Norman Bishop, Odo.

SOURCE 11 King Edward on the throne, and Harold on horseback

1 How reliable do you think these three sources of evidence about Harold are? Explain your answers as fully as you can.
   a The *Anglo-Saxon Chronicles*
   b The *Life of King Edward*
   c The Bayeux Tapestry

2 Do you think Harold had a good claim to the throne?

Edward the Confessor had good reason to hate Harold's family. Edward's brother, Alfred, was killed by them. This event is described in *The Deeds of the Duke of the Normans*, written by William of Jumieges, a Norman monk, in about 1070.

SOURCE 12

'When King Edward's brother Prince Alfred . . . crossed the Sea to Dover . . . the Earl (Godwin, Harold's father) took him into his protection but the same night he had him bound and sent . . . to London . . . When Harold I saw Alfred he at once ordered the Prince to be taken to Ely and there have his eyes put out. And thus the most noble Prince Alfred was done to death without justice.'

---

1 Does Source 10 give the impression that Harold and Edward were close?

2 Does Source 12 throw doubt on this?

3 Source 12 is written by a Norman monk. Should you take this into account when trying to decide how reliable it is?

Claim 3: Harald Hardraada

1 In the 1200s, Snorri Starlasson wrote a Norwegian saga (family story) called *Heimskringla*. Harald Hardraada is written about in it.

SOURCE 13

'At the age of 51, Harald Hardraada was the most renowned soldier of the Age.'

2 Harald was the heir of King Magnus of Norway. Magnus had been promised the throne of England by Canute's son in 1038. The *Chronicles* of 1045 show that, even before Edward the Confessor's death, Magnus took his claim to the English throne seriously:

SOURCE 14

'King Edward gathered a great ship-force on Sandwich because of the threat of Magnus of Norway; but his war with . . . Denmark prevented him coming here.'

SOURCE 15 Sweyn of Denmark (Canute's father) and his army's arrival in England. This illustration is from a 15th century manuscript.

After Edward's death, Harald Hardraada was ready to renew the Norwegian's claim.

3 Harald had the support of Tostig, Harold Godwinesson's younger brother and a leading English earl. Tostig supported Harald, rather than his own brother, because he felt betrayed by Harold. When some of Tostig's tenants had rebelled in 1065 and thrown him off his lands in Northumbria his brother Harold had done nothing to help.

---

1 Do you think Harald Hardraada had a good claim to the throne?
2 Do you think Source 13 is reliable? Explain your answer.
3 Why do you think so many people were keen to become King of England?

Claim 4: William Duke of Normandy

1 William was a distant relative of Edward the Confessor.

2 William was an important and powerful duke.

SOURCE 16

'(When William) took up the arms of Knighthood . . . a tremor ran through all France. Armed and mounted he had no equal.'

Source 16 comes from William of Poitiers' *History of William the Conqueror*, written in the 1070s. Poitiers, a Norman, served William as a knight and as his chaplain.

3 Edward the Confessor had close ties with Normandy. He spent much of his early life there. In 1064, his brother-in-law, Harold, went to Normandy. This is how Poitiers describes the event:

SOURCE 17

'Edward, King of the English, who had already established William as his heir and whom he loved as a brother or a son . . . to confirm his former promise by a further oath sent him Harold who swore loyalty (on the bones of a saint).'

The *Anglo-Saxon Chronicles* make no mention of this visit. In *The Deeds of the Kings of the English*, written in 1125 by William of Normandy, a half-Norman, half-English monk, the journey is described differently.

SOURCE 19

'Harold was at his country seat of Barnham; he went for sport aboard a fishing-boat, and to prolong the entertainment put out to sea. A sudden storm came up and drove him and his companions on the French coast.'

1 Do you think William Duke of Normandy had a good claim to the throne?

2 Sources 17 and 19 disagree in their account of Harold's visit. Which does Source 18 seem to support?

3 Divide the class into 3 groups. Each group should prepare the case for either Harold, Harald or William. Each group should then try to persuade the other groups that theirs is the best claim.

4 a Several different sources have been used in this section. Look back at them and fill in the following table:

Name of Source	Written by	When	Norman/ English

b What difference does the date of the source make to its value to historians?

c Which do you think is the most reliable source?

SOURCE 18 Harold swearing an oath in favour of William

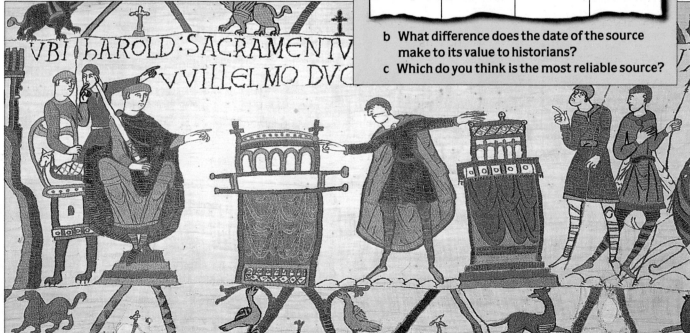

Fight 1: Harold Godwinesson

Chronicon ex Chronicis is a history of the Norman Conquest written by an Anglo-Norman monk between 1090 and 1140. The monk used copies of the *Anglo-Saxon Chronicles* which have since been lost. The *Chronicon ex Chronicis* says:

SOURCE 20

'Harold, son of Earl Godwine, whom the King (Edward) had nominated as his successor, was chosen King by the leading noblemen of all England; and on the same day Harold was crowned with great ceremony by Aldred, Archbishop of York.'

Poitiers tells a different story:

SOURCE 21

'The land of England was without her King Edward, and his crown was worn by Harold. This mad Englishman was not chosen by the people, but seized the royal throne with the help of a few supporters and his broken promise. He was made King by the unholy Stigand.'

Stigand had been unlawfully appointed Archbishop of Canterbury when the previous Archbishop was exiled.

Harold did not have to fight for the throne. The Witan had probably chosen him. But he would have to fight to keep the throne.

1 a Compare Sources 20 and 21. What are the differences between them? Which one does the Bayeux tapestry (Source 22) support?
  b Why do you think the Normans showed Stigand making Harold King?
2 Why do you think the Witan chose Harold and not Edgar Atheling (who was Edward's nearest living relative)?

SOURCE 22 The coronation of Harold from the Bayeux tapestry

Fight 2: Harald Hardraada

Harold realised he would have to fight for the throne. He believed that the greatest threat came from Duke William. So:

SOURCE 23

'When his fleet was assembled, he went to the Isle of Wight and lay there all that Summer and Autumn: and a large land force was kept everywhere along by the sea.'

Anglo-Saxon Chronicles 1066

As provisions grew short and harvest time drew near, Harold's men returned to their homes. Harold also lost part of his fleet in a storm. Then, not William but Harald attacked. He had over 300 ships and 10,000 men under his command. He also had the help of Tostig, Harold's brother, and the men of the Orkneys. These Vikings attacked in the North. They advanced towards York.

SOURCE 24

'Earl Edwin and Earl Morcar assembled from their earldoms as large a force as they could muster, and fought against the invaders and caused them heavy casualties (but) the Norwegians remained masters of the field.'

Anglo-Saxon Chronicles 1066

When Harold was told of the invasion he quickly regathered his forces and marched north day and night.

SOURCE 25

'Harold our King came upon the Norwegians by surprise and met them beyond York at Stamford Bridge with a large force of the English people; and that day there was a very fierce fight on both sides.'

Anglo-Saxon Chronicles 1066

Both Harald Hardraada and Tostig were killed. The *Chronicles* tell how complete Harold's victory was:

SOURCE 26

'The English . . . pursued them until some got to the ships. Some were drowned, and some burned, and some destroyed in various ways so that few survived . . . and the King let them go home with twentyfour ships.'

Reread Sources 23, 24, 25 and 26 carefully.

1 **Do you think the writer of the *Anglo-Saxon Chronicles* supported Harold?**
2 **What do the events described here tell us about Harold as a leader?**

 ## Fight 3: William Duke of Normandy

William was ready to invade England by August 1066, but he was stopped because the wind was in the wrong direction. He sailed on 27 September. Harold was still in the north. He had to rush south to fight William. The two forces met near Hastings, on Senlac Hill. The two armies fought all day, neither side gaining the advantage, until:

SOURCE 27

'The Normans and their allied forces, realising that they could not overcome an enemy so numerous and standing so firm without great loss to themselves, retreated deliberately, pretending flight.'

Poitiers

Some of Harold's men followed and, as a result, the Anglo-Saxon line was broken. Harold was killed, hit by an arrow and then cut down by the Normans. What remained of the Anglo-Saxon army fled.

ACTIVITY

Work in pairs. Look carefully at these pictures from the Bayeux Tapestry which are in the right order. Match each picture to the text on the following page, which is jumbled up, describing the events in the picture.

A

B

ISTI PORTANT:ARMAS: ADNAVE TRAHVN CVMVIN

C

TRAN SIVIT ET VENIT AD PEVENE SÆ

D

DE NAVIBVS · ET HIC:MILITES: FESTINA VERV ANT:HESTINGA: VT CIBVM · RAPERENT

E INPRELIO HIC ODO

F PIENTER AD PRELIUM CON R

G

H DERUN SIMUL ANGLI ET FRANCI INPREL

I RUNT QUI ERANT CUM HAROLDO

J HAROLD

58

1 'They were borne by a favourable wind to Pevensey where they made an unopposed landing.'

Poitiers

2 'Three horses were killed under him (William). Three times he lept to his feet undaunted and swiftly avenged the death of his steed.'

Poitiers

3 'Yet not daring to fight on equal terms with William whom they feared more than the King of Norway, they took up position on higher ground on a hill.'

Poitiers

4 'The Normans, enflamed, surrounded some thousand of those who had pursued them and killed them in an instant.'

Poitiers

5 'Those on foot led the way . . . bearing their bows. The knights rode next, supporting the bowmen from behind.'

Roman de Rou by Robert Wace (Written c 1160)

6 'Duke William . . . quickly caused a fleet of 3,000 vessels to be built.'

Jumièges

7 'The eager courage of the Normans gave them the first strike . . . they threw spears and weapons of every kind.'

Poitiers

8 The ships were 'Loaded both with splendid horses and the finest warriors, with hauberks (coats of mail) and with helmets'.

Jumièges

9 'Then it was that an arrow which was shot towards the sky, struck Harold above the right eye and that one of his eyes it put out.'

Carmen de Hastingensi Proelio by Guy of Amiens (written c 1067)

10 'Thence with a following wind, sails spread aloft he crossed the sea.'

Jumièges

Now answer these questions.

1 **What were the differences between Harold's and William's warriors at the Battle of Hastings?**

2 **Look at the tapestry and write one or two sentences describing the Norman armour, weapons and ships.**

3a **Why do you think Bishop Odo wanted the tapestry made?**

b **Do you think pictures can describe events as powerfully as words?**

c **In England, in the middle of the 11th century, why was it very important to use pictures?**

It was one thing for William to invade England and win the Battle of Hastings. It was quite another for him to conquer the whole of England. Over the next few years William set about making Norman rule in England strong and safe. He did it with great determination, energy and ruthlessness.

Opposition to William

The Anglo-Saxon lords were not going to give up their lands to William and his Normans without a fight. However, with Harold dead and Edgar the Atheling only a child, there was no one to unite them. Southern England was conquered in 1067, the West Country in 1068. Then, in 1069, William faced a major rebellion in the North led by the Anglo-Saxon earls, Edwin and Morcar, with Danish help. William showed no mercy towards these rebels.

SOURCE 29

'He cut down many in his vengence. He destroyed the homes of others, and burnt them to ashes. In his anger he commanded that all crops and herds, property, and food of every kind should be collected together and burnt, so that the whole region north of the Humber might be stripped of everything to support life. As a result, so serious a shortage was felt, and so terrible a famine fell upon the humble and defenceless population that more than 100,000 Christian folk, men and women, young and old, died in hunger'.

Orderic Vitalis—Ecclesiastical History, 1123

Source 30, from the Bayeux Tapestry, shows Normans burning a house before the Battle of Hastings.

SOURCE 30

1. Why did the events shown in Sources 29 and 30 produce a famine?
2. The population of England at that time was about 1½ million. What percentage died in the famine?
3. The population of Britain now is about 56 million. If the same percentage died how many would this be?
4. What do these sources tell you about William?

The last opposition came from Earl Hereward (the Wake). He attacked the Normans from a base at Ely in the wet and marshy fens, in 1071. William built a dry track into the fens and also used ships to defeat him.

Castles

William also ordered castles to be built all over England. You can find out what these castles looked like in the next unit. For William, they did the important job of providing a strong point in each area. With a castle as a base a small number of Norman soldiers could control a large number of Anglo-Saxon peasants.

SOURCE 31 Castles built during William's reign. These are just the ones we know about—there may have been more.

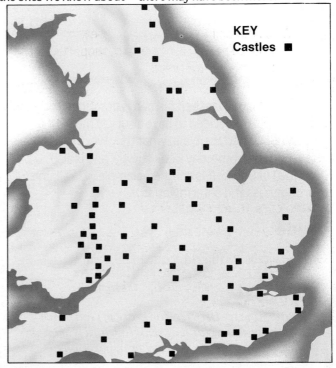

KEY
Castles ■

Land

The Normans who had fought alongside William at Hastings expected to be rewarded with land. William needed soldiers to help him keep England under control. Therefore when William granted land to one of his followers, he made the follower promise to supply him with one or more soldiers, whenever William demanded.

SOURCE 32

Source 32 is a drawing of the system called the feudal system. The King, on the right, gives land to one of his men. This man points to the land which is now his. He also points to himself, showing that he will serve the King as a soldier and clasps hands with the King, swearing:

SOURCE 33

'I will be your man from this day onwards, for life and limb and loyalty. I shall be true and faithful to you for the lands that I hold from you.'

The way the land was then farmed is described in Unit 6. In 1086 William decided to have a survey made of all his lands, who owned them and what they were worth. This was called the Domesday Book survey, and is also described in Unit 6. It is another example of William's thoroughness and determination.

Trade

Orderic Vitalis, writing in about 1123, said:

SOURCE 34

At this time (c. 1070) by the grace of God peace reigned over England . . . English and Normans were living peacefully together in boroughs,

towns and cities, and were intermarrying with each other. You could see many villages or town markets filled with displays of French wares . . . and the English, who had previously seemed contemptible to the French in their native dress, completely transformed by foreign fashions . . .'

Orderic Vitalis

1 Do you think, from what you have read in this unit, that Orderic Vitalis was describing a true picture?

Whether what Orderic Vitalis writes in Source 34 was true in 1070 or not, it was largely true at the time he was writing (1123). England was now closely linked to France in all sorts of ways. The trade links are described in Unit 6, but there were others.

French fashions were worn (Source 34). French words came into the English language (for example, beef, mutton, port, cat, herb, village, flower).

If Harald Hardraada had won at Stamford Bridge in 1066 England would have become part of the Scandinavian world, centred on the Baltic and North Sea. As it was, William won, and England's history became tied up with France and the Mediterranean from then on.

The Church

The Church was a very important part of the way a country was ruled at that time. Most of the cleverest and best-educated people were members of the Church. There was also a church in nearly every village, and villagers took notice of what the priest said. With no newspapers, radio or TV it was the only way most people heard about what was going on outside their village. Kings therefore wanted to make sure the Church was on their side.

William brought over to England church men who were just as determined and vigorous—although not as cruel—as he was. Nearly all the Anglo-Saxon bishops were removed and replaced by Normans. Led by Lanfranc, the new Norman Archbishop of Canterbury, they set about re-organising the Church of England.

One of the first things they did was to build new churches, cathedrals and abbeys. Anglo-Saxon churches had mostly been quite small, often made of wood. The Normans built in stone, whether it was a little parish church, like Barfreston, Source 35 or a great cathedral, like Source 36.

SOURCE 35 Norman Church at Barfreston, Kent

SOURCE 36 Durham Cathedral

ASSESSMENT

Cause and Consequence

1 Historians tend to judge the importance of events by their results. Was the Norman Conquest an important event?

Bias

2 Find an example of a biased source. How could an historian make use of this biased source?

Making use of Evidence

3 Write a short paragraph saying what this unit has taught you about historical *evidence*. You might want to include something on:

  a written and pictorial evidence   b conflicting evidence
  c biased evidence

4 Find examples of:
  a fact
  b opinion
  c judgement
    in the written sources in this unit.

THE RISE AND FALL OF
THE CASTLE

SOURCE 1 An attack on a castle

'My heart is filled with gladness when I see
Strong castles being besieged and the stockades
broken and cracked. . . .
Shields that will be split and shattered as soon
as the fight begins. . . .

A FRENCH POET WROTE the lines on the left in about 1200 AD. Obviously he relished the excitement of a siege. When you look closely at some of the painful scenes in Source 1 you might not be so keen.

Castles were important throughout the Middle Ages, not only in wars, but in peace time too. William the Conqueror had lots of them, built all over England, as we saw in the last unit (Source 31, page 59). He built MOTTE AND BAILEY castles, like the one at Rayleigh, Essex, shown as a reconstruction in Source 2.

SOURCE 2 Reconstruction of Rayleigh castle

The Motte is the high mound at the left with a ditch all round it. There is a little wooden keep on the top of the motte. The bailey is the large enclosure on the right, surrounded by a ditch and a fence. The buildings where the people usually lived were here. Source 3 shows the remains of such a motte and bailey castle. Some castles were gradually added to over the years until they became large complicated castles, or even royal residences, like Windsor (Source 4).

You can still see the motte at Windsor—the mound in the centre. It now has a round stone keep on top, and the castle has two baileys, one on each side. Windsor is an unusual castle because it is still lived in. Most castles are now ruins, and castle ruins can be found all over Britain. If you have visited a few castles you will know that they are often quite different from one another.

SOURCE 3 Remains of a motte and bailey castle

SOURCE 4 Windsor Castle

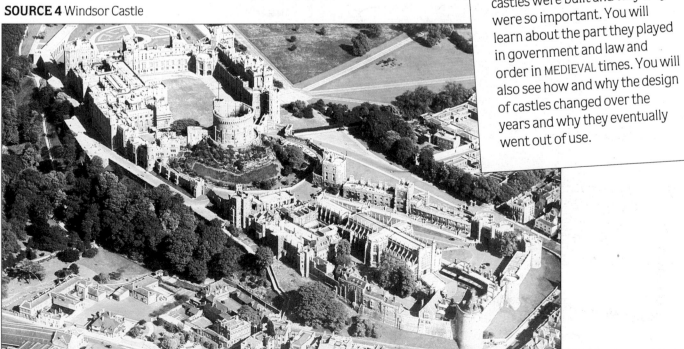

AIMS

In this unit you will find out why castles were built and why they were so important. You will learn about the part they played in government and law and order in MEDIEVAL times. You will also see how and why the design of castles changed over the years and why they eventually went out of use.

Controlling England

As you saw in the last unit, William built motte and bailey castles in order to control his new kingdom. Each one provided a safe base for a small garrison of Norman soldiers. They could keep an eye on the local Anglo-Saxons, and spot any signs of rebellion before any real trouble started.

The castle itself reminded the Anglo-Saxons that they had new masters. The bailey provided a safe residence for the Norman lord for the first few years. He could retire into the safety of the motte if there was any serious trouble.

Governing England

When life had settled down, and the Anglo-Saxons had, reluctantly, accepted Norman rule, castles became the bases from which England was governed. As the king travelled around, he would stay in a convenient local castle. From the great hall of this castle he would give his orders. There he would listen to those who had a problem to put to him, and try serious crimes.

SOURCE 5 The Seal of King Henry II

But the king could not be everywhere. He had few officials to help run the country, no police force to keep order, and no Inland Revenue to collect taxes. All these things were done by his barons from their castles.

The castle at Alnwick, for example, (Source 6) was the home of the Earl of Northumberland. From here the Earl looked after the town of Alnwick and the surrounding county of Northumberland. This was important because it was on the frontier with Scotland, a foreign country until 1603.

SOURCE 6 Alnwick Castle and Alnwick

Even where there was no town, the local castle provided the centre from which the village was run. Source 7 shows the remains of the castle and village of Pleshey, Essex.

SOURCE 7 Pleshey village and remains of the castle

ACTIVITY

THE MANOR COURT

As a class you are going to improvise a drama based on the manor court. Imagine that a manor court is being held in the hall of a castle near you. A few days before, one of the lord's servants comes round telling villagers to attend. If they don't they will be fined. The lord or lady acts as the chairperson of the court, and a clerk writes everything down. Twelve people swear an oath to find out and put before the court anyone who has broken the laws or the customs of the village. Here are some typical laws and customs.

- Everyone had to pay the same tax to the lord.
- Everyone had to give the lord 12 eggs at Easter, or their value in money.
- Everyone had to work for the lord so many days per week plus so many extra days per year.
- No-one could let their animals graze on the lord's land.
- No hut could be built on cultivated land.
- All huts, barns and animal pens had to be kept in good repair.
- All ale, bread or other goods sold in the village had to be of a good standard.

Here are some actual fines from the records of two villages:

SOURCE 8

Alice Walls had to pay a fine of 6d (2½p) in order to be allowed to get married.

All the villagers had to repair the sheep-pen before the next court or pay a fine of 160 shillings (£8)

All the villagers were ordered to keep off the path across the land called Littlemeres in the holding of Henry of Henraw, on a penalty of 12d (5p)

It was ordered that everyone should help look after the pigs when his turn came, on penalty of 12d (5p).

All the villages were ordered not to play football, on penalty of 40 shillings (£2).

You can see that most of the punishments were fines. Sometimes people were punished by being put in the stocks. If someone was sentenced to prison, he would serve this time in the castle dungeon. Why do you think the fine for playing football was so high?

SOURCE 9 A man in the stocks while villagers look on.

What sort of law-breaking would bring the punishment of the stocks, do you think?

Now improvise a drama based on the manor court.

You will need: a lord or lady of the manor, a clerk and about 12 people for a jury. The rest of the class play the villagers. Each jury member names a villager and says which law, or custom, they have broken. The named persons can speak in their defence, but the members of the jury can reply. The lord or lady keeps order and decides if the named person is guilty or not, and what the punishment should be.

Over the years people were always finding new ways of attacking a castle. This led castle-architects to think of new ways of stopping them, which led the attackers to think up new ideas, and so on. For this reason, castles changed a good deal over the 500 years after the Norman Conquest.

Wood and Earth

We have seen the kinds of castles William the Conqueror built. His main aim was to build them quickly. Local people were made to dig the ditches and use the earth for the motte. A wooden fence was put all round it, and the whole thing could be finished in a few months.

Stone and Earth

The kings who followed William were less concerned with speed. It was strength which was more important to them. They therefore started to use stone.

SOURCE 10 The square stone keep of Hedingham Castle

Then the attackers learned how to undermine a castle. A tunnel would be dug under the castle walls. The props which kept the tunnel walls up would be burnt away. The tunnel would then collapse taking with it part of the castle wall. The corners of the square-keeps were the easiest to undermine. Square keeps were, therefore, replaced by round shell keeps, with no corners.

SOURCE 11 Shell keep at Restormel, Cornwall, 12th century

The walls were also made much thicker at the base. Projecting towers were added so that defenders could fire at any attackers who reached the bottom of the walls.

Attackers developed very powerful machines for bombarding the walls of castles. The mangonel could catapult 600lb of rocks. It was powered by the tension of twisted rope. The trebuchet was much more accurate. Its catapult arm was sprung by dropping heavy weights.

SOURCE 12 Mangonel and trebuchet (artist's impressions)

SOURCE 13 Walls of Dover Castle. Notice the thickness of the bases of the towers.

In response, castle builders made the walls even thicker. Dover Castle's walls were over 6 metres thick.

Concentric Castles

Another improvement was brought back to England by Crusaders who had been to the Middle East (see Unit 7). Castles were built with inner ramparts higher than the outer ones, so that archers could fire their arrows from both sets of walls. If attackers broke through one set of wall, they faced another complete circle of walls. These were called CONCENTRIC castles. King Edward I built several of these while he was conquering Wales in the late 13th century, for example, Source 14, Beaumaris Castle.

SOURCE 14 Beaumaris Castle, 1295

Attackers used battering rams to knock holes in the walls or doors and 'bores' to pick away at the brickwork.

SOURCE 15 Battering rams

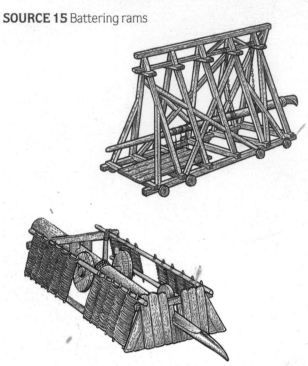

Castle builders therefore started adding special overhanging walkways with trapdoors in the floor through which stones could be dropped onto the rams and bores.

SOURCE 16 Dropping stones on attackers

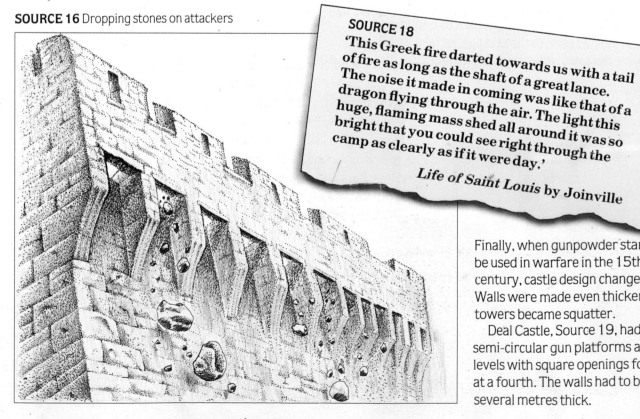

SOURCE 17 Siege tower

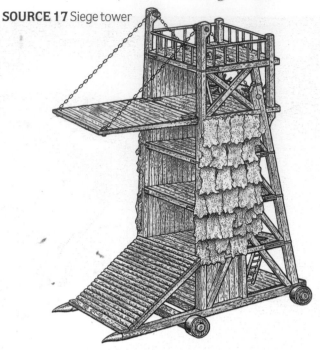

Siege towers or belfries were commonly used in attacks. These were mobile platforms which could be moved right up to the castle wall. They could only be used where the land around the castle was reasonably flat. Castle builders therefore often surrounded the castles with complicated earthworks.

Defenders would use 'Greek fire' against the siege towers. This was a combination of oil, resin, pitch and sulphur.

SOURCE 18

'This Greek fire darted towards us with a tail of fire as long as the shaft of a great lance. The noise it made in coming was like that of a dragon flying through the air. The light this huge, flaming mass shed all around it was so bright that you could see right through the camp as clearly as if it were day.'

Life of Saint Louis by Joinville

Finally, when gunpowder started to be used in warfare in the 15th century, castle design changed again. Walls were made even thicker and towers became squatter.

Deal Castle, Source 19, had huge semi-circular gun platforms at three levels with square openings for guns at a fourth. The walls had to be several metres thick.

SOURCE 19 Deal Castle, 1539

1 Match up the following words and phrases in the left-hand column with the correct definition from the right-hand column.

motte and bailey castle	used to break holes in walls or doors
siege mining	a sort of catapult driven by twisted rope
shell keep	mobile platforms for attackers to reach the castle walls
mangonel	a castle with several walls around it
trebuchet	a thick stone wall enclosing the living quarters of a castle
siege towers	burning oil with other additions
concentric castle	digging under castle walls so they fell down
ram	an early type of castle built by William I
greek fire	a sort of catapult driven by heavy rocks.

2 List 2 advantages and 2 disadvantages of a) wood and b) stone castles.

3 Draw up a table like the one started below and fill it in.

Change in attack methods and weapons	Castles builders' response

RIVALRY BETWEEN KING AND BARONS

Once the Normans were safely in control of England, the barons sometimes refused to obey the king. They were very powerful men, and built large castles of their own to rival the kings'. In Suffolk, for example, the Duke of Norfolk built a large castle at Framlingham while King Henry II was building his castle at Orford, only 20 miles away. Sometimes this rivalry came to war, as at the siege of Kenilworth in 1266.

SOURCE 20 Kenilworth Castle today

Kenilworth Castle was built in the 12th century by Geoffrey de Clinton who was treasurer to Henry I (1100–1135). It was added to by other owners at later dates.

In 1265, Simon de Montfort was living in Kenilworth Castle. He had joined many other English noblemen in a rebellion against the king—King Henry III. He was killed at the Battle of Evesham, but his son, also called Simon, took refuge in the castle, along with the other rebels. Many believed it was impossible to capture Kenilworth. It was almost completely surrounded by over 100 acres of water in pools and meres.

To defeat the rebels, Henry demanded help from all over the realm. Siege engines were sent from Somerset, Gloucester, Worcester, Nottingham and London. Gloucester also supplied siege towers and iron. Lincoln and London sent 30,000 crossbows. Sussex and Surrey sent 300 sheaves of arrows. 2,500 barricades came from Oxford, Worcester and Northampton. The cost was enormous.

The two siege towers, each carrying over 200 crossbow men, were destroyed by a catapult used by the castle defenders. Worried by the cost, the king tried to negotiate with the rebels. When this failed, they were excommunicated by the Archbishop of Canterbury. (This meant they were no longer allowed to be Christians and so would not be able to go to Heaven.) The defenders hit back by dressing up the castle's doctor to look like a bishop. He then excommunicated the king and the Archbishop of Canterbury! Finally, in mid-December 1266, the defenders were forced to surrender because they were short of food and no help had arrived.

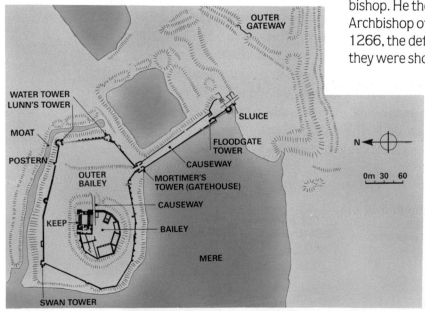

SOURCE 21 Plan of Kenilworth in 1266

Answer in pairs.
1 **Where do you think Henry probably chose to mount his attack from? Why?**
2 **Which different methods were used to capture the castle? Which one succeeded?**

HOW WERE CASTLES BUILT?

A master mason was in charge of building a castle. He was a skilful craftsman. He would design the castle and control its building. Master James of St George was the chief castle builder of Edward I (1272–1307). He was titled 'Master of the kings' works in Wales'. He earned twice as much a day as a knight. He was appointed Constable (in charge) of Harlech Castle. John of Gloucester (another master mason) received, 'Two robes yearly of good squirrel fur, such as the knights of our household receive, plus daily wages, presents of timber and property'.

The master masons were very powerful. Walter of Hereford (who was in charge of the works at Caernarvon) was allowed to hold his own court to try workmen. He kept any fines he imposed!

The workforce was brought by the master masons from all over the country. They were paid but they disliked the work.

SOURCE 22 Building a castle—from a 13th century picture

SOURCE 23
Builth Castle's Labour Force

		Weekly Wage (shown as if it is in today's money)
1	Master mason — 1	22p
1	Deputy mason — 2	15p
4	Masons — 3	10p
5	Masons — 4	8.5p
3	Masons — 5	7.5p
10	Earth clearers/Stone breakers — 6 — 7	5 or 4p
4	Mortar makers — 8	4p
10	Mortar carriers — 9	4p
4	Sand throwers — 10	4p
4	Water carriers — 11	3p
34	Hodmen — 12	3p
30	Diggers — 13	3.5p
20	Barrowmen — 14	3.5p
2	Carpenters — 15	9p
1	Carpenter — 16	8p
1	Smith (sharpener) — 17	10p
1	Smith (sharpener) — 18	6p
2	Foremen — 19	6p
3	Carters — 20	4.5p
36	Women — 21	2.5p

ACTIVITY

Work in pairs. One of you is the master mason in charge of building Builth Castle. The other is the deputy mason. Decide together which of the following jobs are to be done by which labourers.

1 **Clear surrounding area.**
2 **Dig ditches.**
3 **Prepare foundations.**
4 **Build walls and towers.**
5 **Construct wooden buildings inside the walls.**

Compare your choices with those of other pairs.

Builth was a small castle. At Flint over 2,300 diggers were employed. Castles were usually built quickly. Conway with its 22 towers and 3 gates was built in only 40 months.

The great hall was the most important room in a castle. Here most people who lived in a castle slept, ate and spent most of their time. This was because, in the Middle Ages, members of a lord's household were seen as part of a large family. Most castles of any size had a household of over 150. They would all eat together in the hall.

SOURCE 24 The Hall at Penshurst Place (Kent), built in about 1341

As lords became wealthier, the look of the hall changed. The lord's table was placed on a raised platform. The walls were hung with tapestries. They added colour and kept out draughts.

SOURCE 25

'Wretched is the hall . . . each day in the week. There the lord and lady liketh not to sit. Now have the rich a rule to eat by themselves in a privy parlour . . . for poor men's sake, or in a chamber with a chimney and leave the Chief Hall that was made for meals, for men to eat in.'

Langland's Vision of Piers Plowman, written in about 1362

As Source 25 explains, from the mid-14th century, it was increasingly fashionable for the lord, his family and guests to eat separately from the rest of the household.

As castle design became more complex, the lord's family might also have their own private bedroom or sitting room called a 'solar'. There might even be rooms for guests. The floors did not change. There were no carpets, just rushes or straw.

The kitchen also changed considerably. In the earliest castles food was cooked in the open. Again, as castles became more comfortable, the kitchen moved indoors and towards the hall, but away from the lord's private rooms because of the smell.

For this reason too, 'garderobes' or toilets were provided. They were built so that the contents fell into the moat, away from the people living in the castle.

Castles were really like small villages, and even had their own chapels.

Framlingham Castle—Suffolk

c.1100	Site given to Roger Bigod by Henry I.
1306	Castle came under control of Edward III.
1312	Given to the Duke of Norfolk.
1510	Considerable modernization carried out: more windows built in the curtain wall, chimneys added, and a new entrance built.
16th century	Ownership passed back and forth between the King and the Dukes of Norfolk.
1590s	Used as a prison by Queen Elizabeth I.
1635	Bought by Sir R. Hitcham (Merchant)
1636	Given to Pembroke College, Cambridge, on condition that the buildings inside the wall were demolished and it was used as a Poor House.

SOURCE 26 Corfe Castle in ruins

By now, you should have some idea of why castles like Framlingham and Corfe were built. But why did they end up as ruins?

Changes in Warfare

SOURCE 27
'Mons Meg', a cannon of about 1450, kept in Edinburgh Castle

Gunpowder was first used in warfare in Europe in the 14th century. At first the guns were weak and inaccurate, serving only to frighten horses with their smoke and flames. By the 15th century, however, cannon such as Mons Meg could fire a huge iron or stone cannon ball nearly a mile. Clearly all the castles built up to that time were useless against such cannon.

Cannon and hand-guns changed warfare as well. It needed skilled, trained soldiers to fire them. Armies were now made up of mercenaries—full-time, trained soldiers who would use their knowledge for the benefit of anyone who could pay their wages. The knight in armour, turning out to fight for his lord for 40 days per year, was no longer needed. So both the castles, and the knights who lived in them became redundant.

Growth in the Power of Kings and Parliament

Gunpowder and cannon reduced the power of the independent barons. Only the king had the money to buy the cannon and pay the mercenaries. Resistance to kings—like Simon de Montfort's rebellion at Kenilworth in 1266—was no longer possible.

By the 15th century, the end of labour services meant that the manor court was less important (see Unit 8, p.115). The king sent his own judges round the country to try important cases. Less important matters were tried by Justices of the Peace, who were appointed by the king. Taxes were also collected by royal officials. By the 16th century, the Tudor rulers made much more use of Parliament in running the country.

Parliament was made up of the House of Lords, which included bishops, and the House of Commons. The House of Commons contained two knights from every shire (county) and two burgesses from every borough.

SOURCE 28 Parliament of Edward I

In Source 28, find:

a the king   b the bishops   c the lords
d the Lord Chancellor and his clerks sitting on woolsacks

All these changes weakened the power of the barons. The castles, which had been the centres of the barons' power, declined with them.

Better Standards of Living

Only one kind of castle was built in the age of the cannon: this was the 'clover-leaf' type of castle built by Henry VIII along the south coast of England (see Source 19). Deal Castle provided cramped accommodation for just 20 soldiers. Such a low, squat building, with such thick walls gave no room for great halls, kitchens and chapels. They were not the sorts of places barons wanted to live in.

If castles were no longer any use in warfare, then they could be built or altered to be more comfortable. The difference can be seen by comparing Sources 29 and 30.

Barons now wanted smaller rooms, with large windows made of glass. Roaring log fires, with chimneys to take the smoke away, were also a great deal cosier and more civilised than open fires.

SOURCE 29 Stokesay Castle, in Shropshire, late 13th century

Stokesay Castle shows the beginning of this trend: the little round stone keep, on the left, provided a refuge if an enemy attacked. However, the lord and his household lived for most of the time in the Hall, in the centre. His family lived in the pleasant rooms to the top left of the picture. Source 30 shows the type of house many lords were living in by the end of the 15th century.

SOURCE 30 Lytes Cary House in Somerset—1480

In pairs, compare Sources 29 and 30.
a   What are the main differences between the two buildings?
b   Look back at the timeline for Framlingham Castle. In what ways and at what date, was it made more comfortable?

The new houses were no use in war. Often all that remained of their 'castle' origins was the 'crenellation' along the top. This was originally designed as a way of giving archers protection while they fired at attackers. At Lytes Cary in Source 30, it has become little more than decoration above the window. Clearly this house was built for comfort, not to face the battering-ram!

ASSESSMENT

Chronology

Similarity and Difference

1 Here are pictures of 4 different castles (Sources 31–34).
   a Put them in order of construction.
   b Write 2 or 3 sentences describing the main features of each.

SOURCE 31

SOURCE 32

SOURCE 33

SOURCE 34

Change and Continuity

2 Pick out from the boxes below, 3 important reasons why castles were built and 3 reasons why they declined.

Because barons were not so important.

To give the king somewhere to stay when he was travelling around.

To serve as a fortress against rebellions.

Because lords wanted to live more comfortably.

A safe home for a Norman lord.

Because they could no longer be built to withstand attack from cannon.

Because England became more peaceful.

To serve as a centre for ruling the countryside.

SOURCE 1 Woman feeding her hen and chicks, 1340

Village Life ~ Town Life

moutatur mant et pannato uu?.

gaudebunt campi et omnia que in

eis sunt

SOURCE 2 Women and men harvesting wheat, 1340s

OVER 500 YEARS separate the pictures in Sources 2 and 3, yet they look very much the same.

---

1 **What differences can you see? What similarities? Do you think these pictures tell us that England did not change much between 1340 and 1880?**

SOURCE 3 Man stooking wheat, Lincolnshire, late 19th century

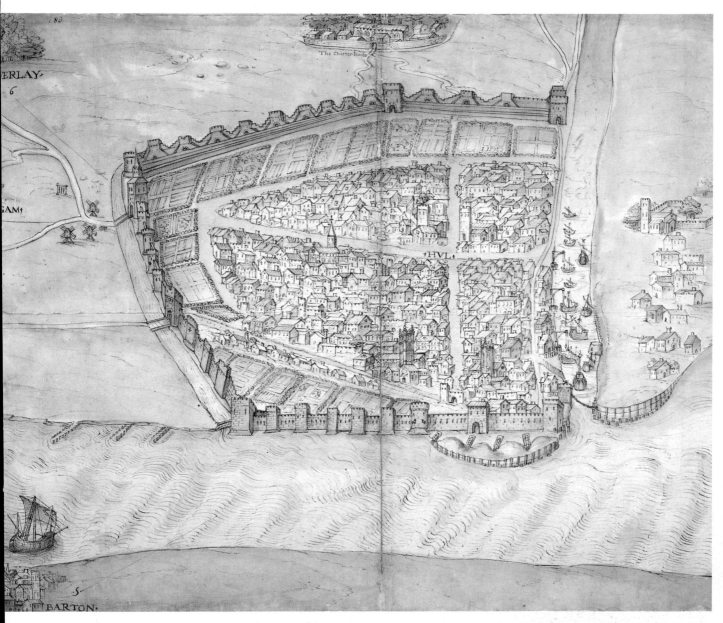

SOURCE 4 Map of Hull at the end of the Middle Ages

There were some towns in the MIDDLE AGES, of course. Hull is now a city and port, with 350,000 people. You can see that in medieval times it was quite small.

> 2 **Look carefully at Source 4. What are the main features of the map? What do you think would be the major differences between medieval Hull and modern Hull?**

AIMS

In this unit you will find out about the people in Sources 1 and 2, the work they did and the hard lives they led. In other units you can read about kings and conquests, castles and crusades. Here you will find out how ordinary people lived and try to understand what it felt like to be a medieval villager. You will be developing your skills of EMPATHY. You will also discover how towns in the Middle Ages grew in size and number, see why this was, and how much towns differed from villages. Again, you will be looking at the people, and trying to understand what it was like to live in a medieval town.

In Unit 4, you saw how William the Conqueror spent many years gaining control of his new kingdom, after his victory at Hastings in 1066. In 1085 he met with his Great Council at Gloucester. Source 5 describes what happened.

> 1 **Write down three things which King William wanted to find out from the survey.**
> 2 **Why would it be difficult to find out these things for every village at that time?**
> 3 **Why is it easier now?**
> 4 **The writer of the *Anglo-Saxon Chronicles* does not seem to approve of this survey. Why do you think this was?**

SOURCE 5

'The King had much thought and deep discussion with his Council about this country . . . Then he sent his men all over England into every shire and had them find out the size of the shire, what land the King himself had, and cattle on the land, and what taxes he ought to have every year from the shire.

Also he caused to be written how much each man had who was a landholder in England, in land or in cattle, and how much it was worth. So very narrowly he caused it to be searched out that there was not a single yard of land, nor even—it is shame to tell, though it seemed no shame to him to do—an ox, nor a cow, nor a swine was left that was not set down in his writing.'

Anglo-Saxon Chronicles

Despite the difficulties, the work was done. William's officials went out to every shire. From every village they called the priest, the reeve (the village foreman who organised the farm work) and six villagers.They met them at the local court and asked them a series of questions. Then a second set of officials came round later to check the information. Amazingly, all this information was collected and written down by the end of 1086. The three biggest towns—London, Bristol and Winchester—were excluded, as were the counties of Cumberland, Northumberland, Durham and Westmorland. Because it was a record that was supposed to last for ever (ie until the day of *Doom* or *Final Judgement*) it was called the Domesday Book. No other country has a survey like it from this period. No other English king carried out such a survey until 1801.

Some Villages in the Domesday Book

Source 6 shows what the entry for one village looks like. It is written in Latin with lots of abbreviations. The translation is given in Source 7. Sources 8, 9 and 10 give the translated entries for three other villages.

SOURCE 6 Domesday Book entry for three villages in Suffolk

SOURCE 7

Suffolk. Sheet 14. Lands of the Abbey of St Edmunds. Thingoe Hundred. St Edmunds held Risby as a manor before 1066. 2 carucates of land. 4 villeins, 2 bordars. Then 2 ploughlands in the demesne, now 4. Always 1 ploughland for the men. Then 3 serfs, now 1. Meadow 1 acre. 3 pack-horses, 12 cattle, 30 pigs, 90 sheep, 32 goats. 7 freeman with 1½ carucates of land. The value of this manor at the time of King Edward £4; now £6.

SOURCE 8

King's Manors. Earl Gyrth held Mutford before 1066. 3½ carucates of land. Always 18 villeins, 6 bordars; then 16 serfs, now 10. Then 4 ploughlands in the demesne, now 3. Always 3 ploughlands for the men. Woodland for 60 pigs. Meadow 6 acres. Then 3 pack-horses, now 2. Always 7 cattle, 160 sheep, 50 goats, 2 beehives.

Another 26 freemen dwell in Mutford, with 2 carucates of land. Always 4 ploughlands. Value 60 shillings, now the same.

SOURCE 9

Richard holds Birmingham of William Fitz Ansculf. There are 6 ploughlands. There is 1 ploughland on the demesne. There are 5 villeins and 4 bordars. There is a wood half a mile long and 4 furlongs wide. In the time of King Edward it was worth 20 shillings, and is still worth the same.

SOURCE 10

Ilkley. The largest part of this manor is waste. Value in 1066 £10. Now £3.

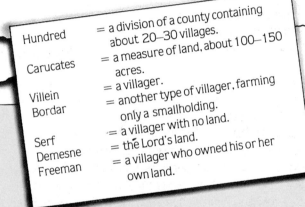

Hundred	= a division of a county containing about 20–30 villages.
Carucates	= a measure of land, about 100–150 acres.
Villein	= a villager.
Bordar	= another type of villager, farming only a smallholding.
Serf	= a villager with no land.
Demesne	= the Lord's land.
Freeman	= a villager who owned his or her own land.

1 **Which village people are NOT mentioned in these entries?**
2 **Why was there so little to record about Ilkley?**
3 **Using the Domesday Book entries, see if you can work out the questions William's officials must have asked. Make a list of these questions.**
4 **What picture of England do you get from these sources?**

You can see that the Domesday Book only had in it the *male* heads of households. Women, children and other relatives were not included. Historians think that the number of villeins, bordars, serfs and freemen has to be multiplied by 4.5 to get the actual population. They calculate that the total population of England in 1086 was about 1½ to 2 million. These people were divided up as follows:

Serfs and their families	11%
Bordars and their families	15%
Villeins and their families	47%
Freemen and their families	23%
King, barons and their families, and members of the church	4%

Yet this last group owned nearly all the land. It was divided up in the following way:

King's lands	17%
300 chief barons' ('tenants-in-chief') lands	54%
Church lands	26%
Anglo-Saxons' lands	3%

The king owned manors in every county of England except Cheshire. Three hundred of the 1500 Normans who came with William to England in 1066 were rewarded with land. Count Robert of Mortain, for example, held 797 manors in 20 counties. The other Normans held manors as tenants of the king, or of his barons. You can see that by 1086, 97% of the land had been taken away from the Anglo-Saxons.

Working the Land

There is only one village in England which now looks anything like villages did in medieval times. It is Laxton in Nottinghamshire.

You can see that the crops are grown in long strips. This is how the fields of every village in the Midlands and southern England would have looked. Villages in northern and western England had small open fields with strips near the village. The rest of the village land, on hillier ground, was open pasture for animals to graze.

Land started to be worked in this way under the Anglo-Saxons in the 5th and 6th centuries. The Normans did not change the system at all. Each villager owned a number of strips scattered among everyone else's all over the open fields. That way everyone got a fair distribution of land—good and not so good. The lord's strips—the demesne—were also mixed up with everyone else's.

The land was worked in strips because of the type of plough that was used (Source 12). You can see that it was very heavy and was pulled by oxen, sometimes by six or eight of them. This made it difficult to turn corners. It was better to run this kind of plough up and down a long strip than round a square field, turning at every corner.

SOURCE 11 Laxton, Nottinghamshire, an aerial photograph.

SOURCE 12 Ploughing in medieval times

The blocks of strips were worked in three fields. Each field had a different use each year. One would grow autumn-sown wheat or rye. Another would grow spring-sown wheat, barley, oats or beans. The third would be left fallow—no crop at all. The following year, the crops would be changed so that the first field had spring-sown crops, the second was fallow, and the third sown in the autumn.

Medieval peasants had no modern fertilizers. They knew that if they grew the same crop on the same land, year after year it would become exhausted. The fallow year was a time for the land to 'rest' and regain fertility. The village animals were grazed on the fallow field, fertilizing it with their manure.

SOURCE 13 Crops and fields over three years (called a 3-year rotation)

Copy this diagram and fill in the blanks with the correct crop for each year.

In the North of England crops were grown on the 'infield', the small fertile fields near the village, every year. Less fertile fields—the 'outfields'—had crops planted every 4, 5, or 10 years.

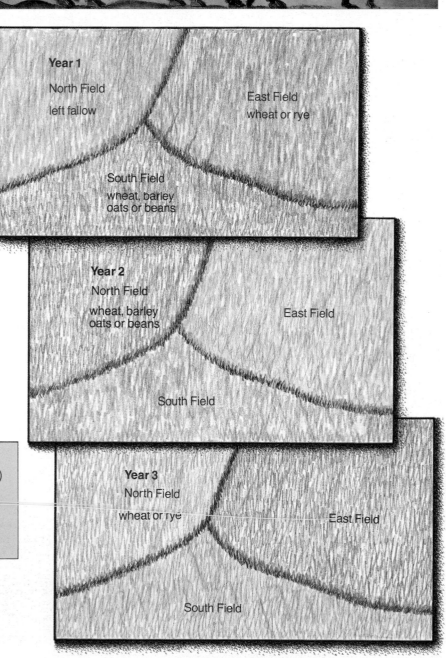

Year 1
North Field
left fallow

East Field
wheat or rye

South Field
wheat, barley oats or beans

Year 2
North Field
wheat, barley oats or beans

East Field

South Field

Year 3
North Field
wheat or rye

East Field

South Field

SOURCE 14 Reeve organising the wheat harvest

This system of farming meant that the village had to work together—plough on the same day, sow the same crop in the same field on the same day, harvest on the same day, and so on. This was all organised by the reeve.

Lord, Church and Villagers

Life was very hard for the villagers. To grow just enough food to live on meant working long hours in the fields. Serfs had no land and no rights at all. Villeins and bordars were not their own masters:

- They did not own their land, but rented it from the lord.
- They paid the rent by working on the lord's strips—the demesne—for three or four days every week. These were called Labour Services.
- They also had to work for the lord for 12 more days every year, doing special jobs such as harvesting or hay-making. These were called boon-days.
- They could not leave the village without permission.
- They could not buy or sell goods.
- They had to pay a fine to the lord when their daughter married.
- A fine had to be paid to the lord when a villein or bordar died, before the heir could take over the land.
- All corn had to be ground in the lord's mill.
- The woods belonged to the lord. A villager could take some firewood, but not cut timber or kill animals.

Freemen didn't suffer from these restrictions. However, they, like everyone else, had to give $\frac{1}{10}$ of their produce to the Church. This was called a *tithe*, and often the Church built huge barns to keep it all in.

SOURCE 15 Tithe-barn at Bradford-on-Avon

Living and Eating

The little huts that medieval people lived in were so small and flimsy that hardly any have survived. Source 16 shows a rather better cottage. There were no windows, as glass was expensive. The floor was made of beaten earth, with an open fire on a stone slab in the middle. There was no chimney, so the cottage was filled with smoke. Peasants had very little furniture—just a few stools, a table and a straw mattress for sleeping. Pigs and chickens often lived in the hut too.

Each hut had a small garden in which the villager could grow a few vegetables. Everything had to be eaten fresh, or else smoked or salted to preserve it. This meant that there was enough to eat in the late summer and early autumn, but supplies were very low by the end of winter. The most common months for deaths were April and May. There was no fodder to feed the animals during the winter, so most of them were slaughtered at Michaelmas (September 29). For a little while, therefore, the villagers had lots of meat. But for most of the year they hardly ate any, apart from a few scraps of smoked or salted bacon or fish. The main drink was ale, or cider.

In the 14th century, the poet William Langland wrote about the shortage of food in the Spring. In Source 17, he tells of Piers Plowman's problems.

SOURCE 16 Cottage in Hampshire

1 What did people live on in winter and spring?
2 What did they have in August and September?
3 Why couldn't they have these things all year round?
4 Langland wrote his poem with each line in two parts, which was the style of his time. Try to write four lines about *your* meals in this style.

SOURCE 17

'I have no penny quoth Piers   pullets for to buy
Nor neither geese nor piglets   but two green cheeses
A few curds and cream   and an oaten cake
And two loaves of beans and bran   to bake for my little ones
And besides I say by my soul   I have no salt bacon
Nor no little eggs, by Christ   collops for to make
But I have parsley and leeks   and many cabbages . . .
And by this livelihood we must live   till Lammas time.'

[The poem goes on to say how, in the late summer, Piers has peascods, beans, baked apples, shallotts, chervils, cherries, pears, leeks, corn, good ale, white bread . . .]

                    'And no piece of bacon
But if it be fresh flesh or fish   fried or baked
And that be warm or hot   to avoid chilling our bellies.'

Pullets	= small chickens	Collops	= a small meal	Lammas = August 1st
Peascods	= pea-pods	Chervil	= aniseed-tasting herb, used in salads

SOURCE 18 Women played an active part in farming.

Women in the Village

Look back at Sources 1 and 2 and at Source 18. They show clearly that women were expected to work in the fields and at the farming tasks. In addition, most jobs in the house were done by the women, such as preparing food, and looking after babies. Children had to work as soon as they could. Many women did some spinning and weaving, making woollen cloth. They either made this into clothes for the family, or sold it to make a little money. 'Gleaning' was done by women. This meant going into the fields after the harvest and gathering any corn that had been missed. They kept this themselves, and made it into flour for bread.

In law, a woman belonged to her father until she married, then to her husband. A 13th century monk ruled that 'a man may chastise his wife and beat her for correction.' A medieval song (Source 19) showed much more sympathy.

SOURCE 21 Women working in the village

SOURCE 19

A woman is a worthy thing
They do the wash and do the wring
Lullay, lullay she doth sing
And yet she hath but care and woe.
A woman is a worthy wight
She serveth man both day and night
Thereto she putteth all her might
Lullay, lullay she doth sing
And yet she hath but care and woe.

People were usually not able to choose their own husband or wife (Source 20). Most girls married at 12–14.

SOURCE 20

'Every year before Shrove Tuesday, when folk are accustomed to think of holy matrimony, the bailiff shall consider what boys and girls are of such an age that they may take wife or husband so that he may allot to each his mate.'

(Bailiff—the lord's representative)

ACTIVITY

Two days in the life of the village

Get into groups of 5. Here are 5 village people. Each member of the group chooses one.

1 The Bordar.
A widow with 2 teenage children. You farm 7 strips and a large garden. This was left to you when your husband died 10 years ago.

2 The Villein.
You farm 28 strips as well as doing all your labour services.

SOURCE 22 Farming in the village

3 The Villein's Wife.
You help your husband on the land, look after your three children, and make cloth. You also keep some chickens, and sell the eggs.

4 The Blacksmith.
You make and repair all the metal tools in the village. This includes the metal tips to the plough-blades. The only horses you shoe belong to the lord. People like to come to your smithy in the winter for a chat as your fire is always glowing hot. You have a cottage with a garden to grow vegetables.

5 The Swineherd
You look after the pigs of the village. They look for food in the woods and wasteland. You are expert at killing the pigs, cutting up and salting the pork.

SOURCE 23 Killing and cutting up pigs

1 Your first task is to write a diary entry, saying what you did one day in September, 1188. Discuss this with your group to get some ideas first. Use all the sources from this unit. Try to think how you would feel doing those tasks, and think how the villagers might have felt. How did they make the hours of work bearable?

2 Write another entry for February, 1189, a winter month. Again try to think how people would have felt. Was there enough to eat?

Why did towns grow?

Almost everything that village people needed to live—their houses, furniture, clothes, shoes, food and drink, were home-made. We can say that the medieval village was 'self-sufficient'. Only salt for preserving food, and iron for knives, ploughshares and metal tools had to be brought in. Lords and their families wanted luxury goods from abroad—spices, wine, furs, silk. The things which did have to be bought, came from a trader at a market. Where there were markets, towns grew up. We have seen that England at the time of the Domesday Book was a land of villages. Even Birmingham was only a village. There were towns too though, even in Anglo-Saxon times (see Unit 2 Source 5). However, apart from London, Bristol, Winchester and Norwich, hardly any town had over 10,000 people. Many had barely 1,000.

ACTIVITY

Siting a Town

Towns sometimes grew up where there was a castle to protect the merchants, or a monastery to encourage travellers. But they were mainly on important routes, especially where these routes crossed.

This map shows four possible sites for a town—A, B, C and D. In the table there are five things which need to be thought about when siting a town. Copy out the table and give each site a mark out of five for each of these things. The best site for a town is the one with the highest total mark.

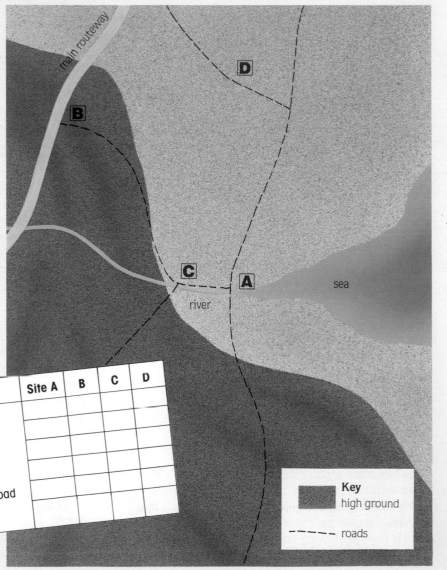

	Site A	B	C	D
Near to water				
On a road				
Safe from attack from the sea				
Near to several villages				
Add a bonus mark if on a cross-road				
Total				

Key
high ground
------- roads

During the Middle Ages towns grew in size, and many new ones grew up. There were several reasons for this. After the Conquest, Britain settled down to a generally peaceful life. The population was rising, so there was more demand for goods. Villagers came into towns to sell their surplus produce—eggs, butter, cheese, vegetables etc. Craftspeople in towns began to specialise in making things to sell to villagers—shoes, gloves, household utensils, leather goods, high quality cloth. Better-off villagers began to buy these things instead of making them themselves.

Lords were keen to set up towns because they made money out of them.

SOURCE 26 Market cross at Ripley, North Yorkshire

SOURCE 24 Customs of the City of Winchester

'No butcher or other person may have a stall in the High St without paying the due to the city.

Every cart that comes into the city with fish for sale owes rent of a half-penny.

Every cart that brings iron or steel, twopence, a horseload one penny.

Every tanner that holds a stall in the High St owes for the ground-rent two shillings.'

More and more lords set up markets in their villages, hoping they would prosper and grow into towns (Source 25). Sometimes they built a market-cross (Source 26) for villagers and traders to set out their goods. Later they might build a market-hall (Source 27). Here the ground-floor was open, so that the stalls could be set out and protected from the weather. The room above was where the Council met.

SOURCE 25 Map of markets in Suffolk 1100–1350

SOURCE 27 Market hall at Ledbury

1 What are the most important things that strike you about each of these sources?
2 What do these sources tell you about town life in medieval England?

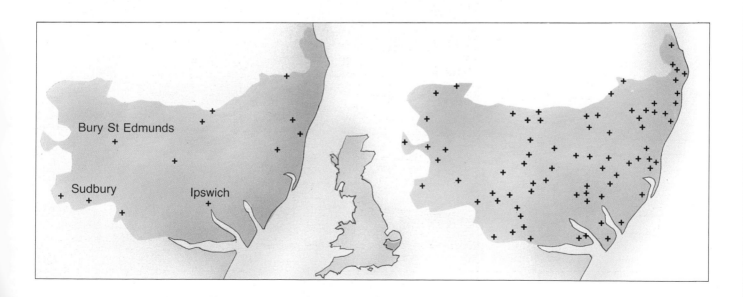

Bury St Edmunds

Sudbury

Ipswich

Some towns did well, attracted people, and grew. Source 28 shows Devizes, Wiltshire. Here the lord gave up first the outer bailey, then the inner bailey of the castle for streets and a market. Some markets did not grow into towns. Source 29 shows New Buckenham, Norfolk, also next to a castle, but never more than a village.

SOURCE 28 Devizes in Wiltshire. This grew into a town very quickly.

SOURCE 29 New Buckenham in Norfolk did not grow into a town.

Trade

As the medieval period went on, the amount of trade increased. English merchants not only travelled all over the country, but traded with much of Europe too. Source 30 shows the kinds of things English merchants bought, and where they came from. The main goods sent out of England to pay for all these things were wool and cloth.

The map also shows that almost all of the goods came by sea. Source 31 shows two of the ships that were used. It also shows a packhorse. The two buildings with signs hanging out are both inns.

SOURCE 30 Overseas trade of England, 15th century.

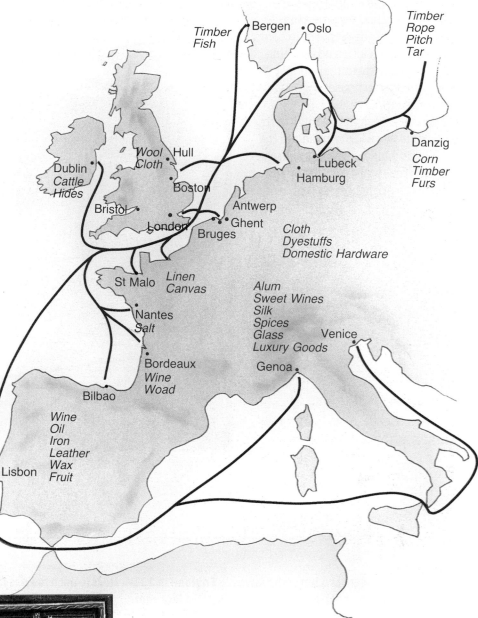

SOURCE 31 Ships and packhorse, about 1400

1 How do these ships compare in size with merchant ships today?
2 How would this small size help them reach inland towns?
3 Why was a packhorse a better way of carrying goods than a horse and cart?

By the end of the Middle Ages, the cloth industry had become a big international trade. Some merchants in the wool and cloth trade became very rich. They spent their money on building splendid houses for themselves (Source 32).

The main areas to benefit from the cloth trade were East Anglia and the Cotswolds. Many of the fine churches in those areas were re-built, or added to, with the profits of the cloth trade.

SOURCE 32 House of Thomas Paycocke, cloth merchant, at Coggeshall, Essex. Paycocke died in 1461.

ACTIVITY

Here is a list of the towns in England in 1334. Next to each town is the amount of tax each paid to King Edward III in that year.

	£
Boston	1,100
Bristol	2,200
King's Lynn	770
Lincoln	1,000
London	11,000
Newcastle	1,333
Norwich	946
Oxford	914
Salisbury	750
Shrewsbury	800
Yarmouth	1,000
York	1,620

In pairs:

1 Arrange the towns in order, starting with the richest.
2 Mark them on a blank map of England. Draw a column next to each town to show its wealth (scale : 1 cm = £1000).
3 Which of the towns are seaports (a short way from the sea)?
4 Which of the towns are river ports?
5 Which parts of England are most of the 12 towns in?
6 Why do you think there are so few of these towns on the West Coast of England?

Look at the list of restrictions on the life of a villein on page 82. Obviously villeins could not be traders. Traders needed to be able to travel freely, to own goods, and buy and sell them. From Anglo-Saxon times, townspeople had been given the freedom to do these things. These free townspeople were called burgesses.

There was a saying 'town air makes you free'. Villeins could become free if they stayed in a town for a year and a day. Towns were therefore quite different for the people who lived in them. They were little islands of freedom in the sea of lords and villeins.

There were several rights which the town wanted from their lord in order to run their own affairs. The first was the right to hold a market, but there were others: the right to collect tolls from outsiders; the right to set up their own court; even the right to have their own Town Council. These rights were granted by a *charter*—a document listing the new rights and freedoms.

SOURCE 34 Apprentice glassblowers

SOURCE 33 Townspeople receiving a charter (15th century)

Trades

Many different jobs and crafts were carried on in towns. In villages everyone knew everyone else, so surnames were not needed. Towns were bigger, so surnames were needed to tell the difference between Anne the Baker (Anne Baker), and Anne the Taylor (Anne Taylor). Some surnames are obvious, like these, and Butcher, Glover, Sadler, and Thatcher. Others are less obvious: Mason—A builder in stone, Fletcher—made arrows, Cooper—made barrels, Scrivener—wrote letters for people.

Each trade was organised in much the same way. A master who was skilled in a particular trade and who ran a business, would take apprentices. These were young people, aged about 12 or 13, who were bound to work for their master, and to learn the trade, for seven years. They were paid very little, and usually lived in the master's house, as part of the family. At the end of their apprenticeship they had to make something to show that they had learnt all the skills of their trade. This was called a masterpiece.

The young person could now become a skilled worker, paid by the day, called a journeyman (French—journée = a day). If you had enough money you could set up on your own, as a master.

In many towns, the craftspeople in a particular trade would all join together in a guild. They paid a small subscription, and it was something like a trade union. Here are some of the things a guild did:

SOURCE 35
'If it so happens that any of the members became poor, through old age, or through any other chance, through fire or water, thieves or sickness . . . then the member shall have 6d (2½p) per week, from the common box.'

Tanners Guild of London.

SOURCE 36
'If the threads in the cloth are too far apart, the cloth and the instrument on which it was made, to be burnt.'

Rules of the Guild of Bristol Weavers.

SOURCE 37
'In the City of Chester a shoemaker, William Guild, was fined the sum of £10 by the guild warden for very poor work. Also all his goods were forfeit.'

Shoemakers Guild of Chester.

SOURCE 38
'On the feast of Corpus Christi all members shall come together to the guild feast.'

Rules of St Michael's guild, Lincoln

These guild feasts could be quite big occasions. At one feast at Salisbury the guild members ate: 10 lambs, 2 calves, 16 pigs, 70 chickens and 100 pigeons.

> 1 How did the guilds look after their members?
> 2 Why did the guilds punish bad work?

At first tradespeople sold their wares from temporary stalls, set up in the street (see Source 39). In time, permanent buildings were built, like Source 40. These usually had a shop on the street with open windows.

SOURCE 39 Open stalls, of a tailor, a barber, a furrier and a grocer.

SOURCE 40 An apothecary's shop. An apothecary was a chemist, selling rare and expensive medicines and potions.

Behind the shop was the workshop where the apprentices and journeymen made the things to sell. Behind that again was the house where the master lived, with his or her family and apprentices. There were also sheds, for raw materials, and a small garden.

> 1 Which stall is which in Source 39?
> 2 Why do you think the apothecary would want a proper shop, not just a stall?

Every trader wanted a shop on the main street, with some space behind to live and work. This meant that towns were laid out with long, narrow, 'burgage plots', running at right angles to the street (see Source 41a). These can still be seen in many towns, even where a modern shop has been built on the front.

SOURCE 41a Drawing of medieval Alnwick, Northumberland, showing burgage plots.

Alnwick had a large triangular market place as you can see in the drawing, with burgage plots running back from each side. Later the market triangle was built over. The town was protected by a castle, and strong gates were built on the main roads into the towns in case of attack.

SOURCE 41b 20th century aerial photograph of Alnwick. The burgage plots can still be seen.

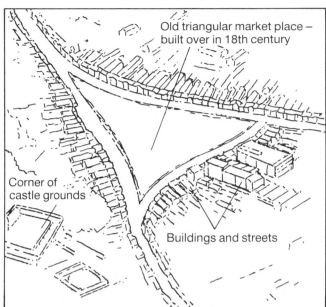

Old triangular market place – built over in 18th century

Corner of castle grounds

Buildings and streets

ACTIVITY

The Town of Imchester

This is a class activity. One-third of the class are stall-holders at a market in a medieval town. The others are customers.

Stall-holders

Several trades have been mentioned already for you to choose from. Here are some more. It doesn't matter if more than one person chooses the same trade—but it could mean having to lower your prices to compete with your rivals:

Fishmonger	Shoemaker
Potter	Sadler
Spicer	Vintner (sold wine)
Draper	Haberdasher (sold small items
Goldsmith	like shoelaces, beads, thread,
Butcher	pegs, toys)
Tailor	Hatter
Furrier	Barber
Baker	

Customers

Decide who you are going to be. You could be:

a villager, coming into town to sell some eggs and buy some salt
a rich lord or lady
a burgess, looking for a present for a friend's birthday
an apprentice, looking for a present to take home to your mother
a foreigner, looking for local goods
a priest, doing the daily shopping
a nun, shopping for the rest of the members of your nunnery
the constable, making sure the law is kept

Here are some other things to remember:
Prices would be much lower than they are today. For example:

Fish:	best mackerel ½p each
	pickled herrings 1p a pound
	wriggling eels, all fresh 25 for 1p
Cloth:	Velvet £1 an ell (an ell measures from finger tip to the opposite shoulder—about 112 cms)
	Satin 33p an ell
	Linen 20p an ell
Haberdashery:	2 dozen red leather shoelaces 3p
	1 string of jet beads 2½p (jet is a shiny black stone)
	1 green leather purse 2½p
	2 pounds of thread 10p

Noises	The market place could be very noisy, with people shouting their wares and trying to sell things. Many prices would be argued over.
Smells	Some nice smells—bread, spices, leather
	Some nasty smells—the tannery, bad fish, bad meat

1 *Stallholders* set up your stalls and decide what you want to sell, at what prices. *Customers* decide what you want to buy. Your teacher will then declare the market open.

2 After a little while an entertainer appears. (Perhaps one member of the class can do handstands, or juggle.) Everyone stops to watch. Someone steals something off a stall. The entertainment ends and everyone gives the entertainer a penny. Then the theft is discovered. The constable has to investigate.

3 One of the customers accuses one of the traders of unfair dealing (short measure, shoddy goods, bad food etc). An argument breaks out. The constable calls both people to the Court of Pie-Powder—the market court. This consists of six stallholders and six customers. They hear both sides, then make a decision.

Here are some of the punishments that were handed out by the market court at Salisbury:

SOURCE 42

'John Penrose sold unsound and unwholesome red wine. He was condemned to drink some of the same wine and have the rest poured over his head.'
'John Russell sold 37 pigeons all bad. He had to stand in the pillory and have the pigeons burnt underneath.'

The pillory was a frame with holes to hold the neck and wrists of the criminal. Stocks held criminals' ankles. Both were used by the Court of Pie-Powder.

4 *Writing-up.* Each person must now write an account of market-day in Imchester. Try to think what people felt about the market in *those* days, not what we may feel *now*.

Empathy

1 Imagine you are an apprentice who has just done 6 months working for a master-baker in the nearest town. It is Christmas and you return home to the village where your father and mother live, for the festivities. Your father is a villein.

  a How does your working life compare with your parents'?

  b What hopes and fears do each of you have for the future?

  c What can you tell your parents about town life?

  d What can they tell you about life on the land under a lord?

Write your answers by making up an imaginary conversation between yourself and your family.

Similarity/ Difference

2 a Compare Sources 12 and 44. What are the similarities between these two pictures? What are the differences?

  b Compare Sources 40 and 43. What are the similarities between these two pictures? What are the differences?

  c Neither of the scenes in Sources 43 and 44 would be seen today. This seems to suggest that there has been more change since 1900 than in the 500–600 years before that. Do you agree with this? Why do you think this is so?

SOURCE 43 Shop in Whitby, about 1900

SOURCE 44 Team of oxen, about 1900

The Crusades ~

ON 7 SEPTEMBER 1191 King Richard of England was marching south along the coast of the Holy Land. He was at the head of a large army of Crusaders who wanted to recapture Jerusalem from Saladin (Salah-ud-din), leader of the Turks.

SOURCE 1 Crusader knight

SOURCE 2 Turkish Warrior

SOURCE 3 A portrait of Saladin by an Egyptian artist

Clashes between Moslems and Christians

Saladin's army was waiting in ambush. A soldier in Richard's army, present at the ambush, described what happened:

SOURCE 4

'It was nearly nine o'clock when there appeared a large Turkish army, ten thousand strong. They came down on us at full charge, throwing spears and arrows as fast as they could, while their voices mingled in one terrible yell . . . In an irresistible charge, their horses faster than eagles and urged on like lightning, they attacked our men. The whole sky was darkened. Our men lost many horses, killed by their spears and arrows. As the enemy lines advanced our bowmen did their best to hold them back. When the Turks came close and the bows could not be used, they fought hand to hand using lances and clubs. The blows of the Turks, echoing from their metal armour, resounded like a hammer striking an anvil. When six trumpets sounded our men in the front line made a united and furious charge, others rushed swiftly onward in one large body. Each troop showed its bravery and advanced on the Turks, spearing them with their lances and knocking them to the ground.

The sky grew dark from the dust thrown up in the battle. The Turks who had dismounted, to use their bows, were surrounded and killed in the charge. Those who our cavalry knocked down were beheaded by the foot soldiers. The rest of the Turkish army retreated and for two miles nothing could be seen but the fleeing enemy.'

SOURCE 5
Crusaders and Turks from an 18th century drawing of a mid-12th century stained glass window which was in the Church of St Denis.

This was the battle of Arsuf. Saladin lost over 7,000 men, Richard only 700. Richard marched on to Jerusalem, but never succeeded in capturing the city from Saladin.

AIMS

In this unit you will be looking in detail at why the Crusades took place. You will find out about the different ideas and beliefs of the Crusaders and the Turks and you will see how these differences were caused by a clash of religious beliefs and a clash of cultures. Finally, you will study some of the consequences of the Crusades.

1 Look at Sources 1 and 2. List the main similarities and differences, between the Turkish warrior and the Crusader.
2 Look at Source 5 and reread Source 4. Which are the Crusaders in the drawing and which are the Turks? How do you know?

3 Why do you think Richard I of England and his army were called *Crusaders*? Why do you think Richard was fighting against the Turks? What were his motives? What 'crusade' do you think they were waging? You may discuss this in pairs.

A Clash of Religions

Almost 100 years before Richard's battle with Saladin, on 18 November 1095, the Pope, Urban II, gave a speech at Clermont in France. This speech marked the beginning of the Crusades.

SOURCE 6 Pope Urban II giving a speech at Clermont. This is taken from a 19th century engraving.

SOURCE 7 Pope Urban's speech. This is taken from a 15th century engraving.

There are four accounts of the speech:

1   The first was written in 1100–6 by Fulcher of Chartres, a chaplain who was at Clermont.

2   The second was written before 1107 by Robert of Rheims, a monk who was at Clermont.

3   The third was written before 1108 by Guibert of Nogent, an abbot who was not at Clermont.

4   The fourth was written in about 1108 by Baldric of Bourgueil, an abbot who was at Clermont.

None of these accounts is believed to be entirely accurate, but by combining them (as in Source 8) we get an idea of how the Pope 'launched' the Crusades.

SOURCE 8

Those present (mostly men of the Church) were told:

'A grave report has come from the lands around Jerusalem and from the city of Constantinople . . . that the Turks, a foreign race, a race absolutely alien to God . . . have invaded the land of those Christians', **2** 'slaughtering and capturing many, destroying churches and laying waste the Kingdom of God.' **1** The Pope warned: 'The end of the world is near. The days of the Devil are at hand. If when he comes he finds no Christians in the East, as at this moment there are none, then truly will there be no man to stand up to him'. **3** He reminded them: 'Your ancestors destroyed the Kingdoms of the Turks and extended into them the boundaries of Christianity'. **2** He told them: 'Until now you have fought unjust wars: you have savagely used spears against each other, killing for greed and pride, for which you will go to hell!' **3** 'Take the road to the Holy Land and rescue it from a dreadful race and rule over it yourselves, for that land as Scripture says, floweth with milk and honey.' **2** 'All men going there who die untimely deaths, whether on the journey, by land or by sea, or while fighting Turks, will immediately have all their sins forgiven'. **1** 'And everyone who has decided to make this holy pilgrimage . . . must wear a cross on his front.' **3** Pope Urban turned to the bishops and other men of the Church and said, 'Proclaim this message in your churches and give your whole voice to preaching this crusade'. **4** The crowd shouted 'Deus le volt!' (God wills it) and some rushed to join the crusade. As the news spread, crusader armies were created all over Europe.

---

1 Look at the four sources of Pope Urban's speech. Can you say which will probably be the most accurate? Why? What other questions might you ask about these sources before using them to write an account of Urban's speech?

2 Compare Source 6 (a 19th century engraving) and Source 7 (a 15th century engraving). What are the main differences? Source 8 contains a clue which points to one engraving being more accurate than the other. What is the clue and which engraving does it tend to support?

Time line showing some of the main events of the Crusades:

1071	The Seljuk Turks crush the Byzantines at Malazgerd and seize Asia Minor. They soon control the entire Holy Land.
1099	*First Crusade*. Christians recapture Jerusalem.
1144	Turks recapture region of Edessa.
1146	*Second Crusade* led by Louis VII, King of France and Conrad III, Emperor of Germany.
1148	Crusaders are defeated at Damascus.
1187	Saladin captures Jerusalem and most of the Holy Land.
1189	*Third Crusade*.
1192	King Richard of England makes peace with Saladin after he fails to recapture Jerusalem.
1204	*Fourth Crusade*. French knights plunder and burn Constantinople without reaching the Holy Land.

1212	*Children's Crusade*. 30,000 children from France and Germany set off for Jerusalem. They fail to reach the Holy Land and thousands are sold into slavery.
1217	*Fifth Crusade*. Three-year campaign fails to capture Egypt.

1228	*Sixth Crusade*. Emperor Frederick II regains Jerusalem by diplomacy.
1243	Moslems recapture Jerusalem.
1248	*Seventh Crusade* led by Louis IX of France. Most of the army is eventually captured.

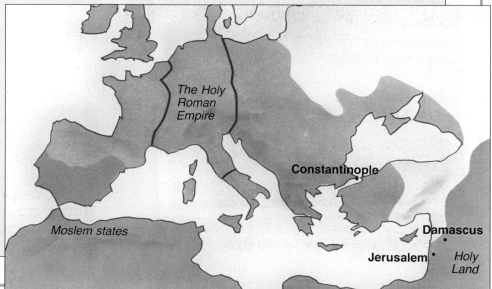

The Holy Roman Empire

Constantinople

Moslem states

Damascus

Jerusalem • Holy Land

Pope Urban II called for a HOLY WAR (or JIHAD). This idea of a holy war has also been used in modern times.

SOURCE 9

Moslems declare holy war on Afghan regime

By Bruce Loudon in Islamabad.

Fierce fighting has been reported in Afghanistan since Islamic 'Holy Fighters' declared a holy war against the communist regime of President Noor Mohammad Tarraki last week. 'Our men are fighting with rifles in one hand and the *Koran* in the other', a Moslem priest from Afghanistan said to me.

'They are fighting a pagan regime which has no place in Afghanistan. The Jihad will surely mean the end of the communists and the triumph of Islam, just as it has triumphed in Iran and Pakistan.'

From *The Daily Telegraph*, March 14 1979

SOURCE 10 Ruthless fighters of Afghanistan, from *The Times* December 23 1980

ACTIVITY

THE BACKGROUND TO THE CLASH

Imagine you are a reporter living in the twelfth or thirteenth century. Use the information which follows to write a short article, explaining why Jerusalem and the Holy Land are so important both to the Turks and to the Christians. Try to say in your article whether you can see any way to solve the dispute.

SOURCE 11 13th century map showing Jerusalem at the centre of the world

In his speech, Pope Urban said:

SOURCE 12

'Jerusalem is the navel of the world, a land fruitful above all others, like a second paradise of delights. The Redeemer of the human race made it famous by his birth, embellished it by his life, sanctified it by his passion, redeemed it by his death, left his seal upon it by his burial.'

Robert of Rheims

Richard wrote in a letter to Saladin:

SOURCE 13

'As far as we are concerned, there are only three subjects of disagreement: Jerusalem, the True Cross and territory. As for Jerusalem, it is our place of worship, and we will never agree to renounce it, even if we have to fight for it to the last man. As for territory, all we want is that land west of Jordan to be given to us. As for the True Cross, for you it is merely a piece of wood, whereas for us it is priceless. Let the Sultan give it to us and let us stop fighting.'

Saladin in a letter to Richard, explained why Jerusalem was equally important to Moslems:

SOURCE 14

'The city is as holy to us as it is to you: it is even more important to us, because it was there that our Prophet made his miraculous journey, and it is there that our people will be reunited on Judgement Day. It is, therefore, out of the question for us Moslems to abandon it. As for territory, this land has always been ours, and your occupation is only temporary . . . So long as there is war we will not allow you to enjoy your possessions. As for the Cross we will use it as a bargaining counter and exchange it for something of value to the Moslem world.'

SOURCE 16 Christ on a donkey and Mohammed on a camel. From an early 14th century Turkish history book.

Moslems believe that Moses and Jesus were prophets of God (Allah), but that it was Mohammed who was chosen by God to complete their preaching. They believe that the Dome of the Rock was where Mohammed had an important vision.

Christians had always flocked to the Holy Land to pray in the holy places. In 638 Moslem armies conquered this area. Life for Christian pilgrims became more difficult although they were still able to travel to the Holy Land. In 1071, however, a new Moslem ruler, Malik Shah, leader of the fierce Seljuk Turks conquered the area. Now Christian pilgrims risked their lives if they journeyed to the Holy Land. As Urban said:

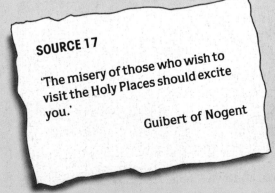

SOURCE 17

'The misery of those who wish to visit the Holy Places should excite you.'

Guibert of Nogent

SOURCE 15 The Dome of the Rock in Jerusalem, built by Byzantine craftsmen for a Turkish leader in 691 AD. Crusaders mistakenly believed it to be the Temple of Solomon.

Although the main reason for the Crusades was to recapture the Holy Land, the Church had other reasons also for being so enthusiastic about the Crusades.

A Way to Reunite the Church

The Turks, as well as capturing the Holy Land, had also defeated the Byzantine army. Byzantium was an important Christian Empire in the East. The Emperor Alexius asked the Pope for help to defeat the Seljuks. As well as helping fellow Christians the Pope hoped to reunite the Church. Christians in the East did not recognise the Pope as head of the Church.

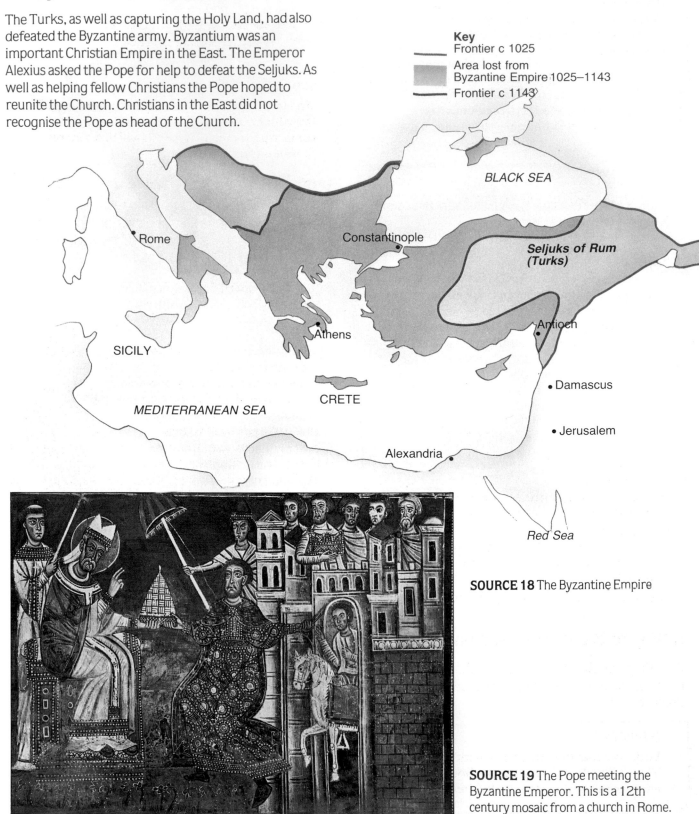

Key
— Frontier c 1025
☐ Area lost from Byzantine Empire 1025–1143
— Frontier c 1143

BLACK SEA

Rome

Constantinople

Seljuks of Rum (Turks)

Athens

SICILY

Antioch

• Damascus

CRETE

• Jerusalem

MEDITERRANEAN SEA

Alexandria

Red Sea

SOURCE 18 The Byzantine Empire

SOURCE 19 The Pope meeting the Byzantine Emperor. This is a 12th century mosaic from a church in Rome.

A Way to Restore the Influence of the Church

Pope Urban said:

> ### SOURCE 20
> *'Stop these hatreds among yourselves, silence the quarrels, still the wars and settle your disagreements.'*
>
> *Robert of Rheims*

This points to another reason for the Church's enthusiasm for the Crusades. The Church felt it was loosing influence over people's lives. It had called a 'truce of God' to try and stop fighting between Christian countries, but this had failed. It hoped that by organising the Crusades it would be able to re-establish its authority over people's lives.

The Church was surprised by the response to its call. What caused people to respond so enthusiastically to the Church's call?

A Way to Spiritual Gain

This letter written by St Bernard of Clairvaux in the 1140s shows one reason why the Crusades were so popular:

> ### SOURCE 21
> **'Oh mighty soldier, oh man of war, you now have a cause in which to win is glorious and for which to die is but to gain. Or are you a shrewd businessman, a man quick to see the profits of this world? If you are, I can offer you a splendid bargain. Do not miss this opportunity. Take the sign of the cross and at once you will have indulgences (forgiveness) for the sins which you confess. It does not cost you much to buy and if you wear it with humbleness you will find it is worth the Kingdom of Heaven.'**

A Way to Wealth and Adventure

Pope Eugenius III, when proclaiming the Second Crusade in 1146, pointed to some of the other benefits of joining a Crusade:

> ### SOURCE 22
> **'We decree that their (the Crusaders') wives and children, goods and possessions should remain under the protection of the Holy Church.'**

> **'All those who are in debt and undertake so holy a journey with pure hearts need not pay interest on past loans.'**

The Abbot Martin of Paris had this to say when he preached about the Crusades in 1201:

> ### SOURCE 23
> **'The land for which you are making is richer by far than this one and more fertile; and it could easily come to pass that many of you will find a more prosperous way of life there.'**

Some knights joined the Crusades in search of adventure. There were many younger sons of noblemen who were bored and stood no chance of inheriting their fathers' lands.

> ### SOURCE 24
> **'. . . I, Nivelo, raised in nobility of birth which produces in many people a dishonourable mind, for the forgiveness of my sins (I) renounce for ever in favour of (the Village of) St Peter wrong behaviour . . . Whenever the onset of knightly savagery stirred me up I used to enter St Peter taking with me a troop of my knights and a crowd of my attendants, and wrongly I would take the goods of the men of St Peter for food for my knights . . . And so since, in order to obtain the Pardon for my crimes which God can give me, I am going on a pilgrimage to Jerusalem . . . the monks have given me £10 . . . towards expenses . . . and they have given £3 to my sister . . . in return for her consent.'**
>
> Written in about 1096

1 Write a letter from the Pope to one of his bishops explaining why the Church is in favour of the Crusades.

2 Look at Source 24. What made Nivelo join the Crusades?

The Crusades were not just a series of 'holy' battles and a clash of religions. Behind them there also lay a clash of cultures. To understand what is meant by a clash of cultures, we need to look at what the Turks and European Crusaders thought of each other.

Sa'id al-Andalusi, a Moslem scientist living in the eleventh century, made a list of all the people of the world in order of their intelligence and ability. He put the Franks (this is what the Moslems called the Crusaders) at the bottom of the list:

> **SOURCE 25**
>
> 'These people study no science and are more like animals than human beings. Those who live in the deep north (England) . . . have been so affected by their extreme distance from the sun . . . resulting in a cold climate and damp air, that their manner has become chilly and their state of minds simple. Consequently their bodies are huge, their colour pale and their hair long. For the same reason they lack keenness in intelligence and they are ignorant and stupid.'

SOURCE 26 12th century illustration showing two Moslem doctors discussing their patients' illnesses.

Usamah-ibn-Munguidh, a Moslem poet, records a case of the Franks' ignorance and brutality:

> **SOURCE 27**
>
> A doctor was asked to cure a knight and an old woman. He tells what happened: 'They brought before me a knight in whose leg a boil had grown and a woman who had gone mad. To the knight I applied a hot dressing with herbs until the boil opened and he became well; and the women I put on a special diet. Just then, a Frankish doctor came along and, pushing me aside he provided his own cures. He said to the knight: 'Which would you prefer, living with one leg or dying with two?' He replied 'Living with one'. The Frankish doctor asked for 'a strong man with an axe'. The knight's sore leg was placed on a block and the axeman cut it off. But the first blow only cut the thigh bone and a second and third blow had to be struck – the marrow of the leg flowed out and the knight promptly died. The Frankish doctor then turned to the women who he had fed on garlic and mustard and had her hair shaved off. When her fits returned (no wonder!) the doctor yelled that she had the devil inside her, he then cut a cross into her forehead with a razor. The women died within a few days.

What really annoyed the Moslems was the Franks' belief that they were far superior to the Moslems. Usamah tells of this attitude in a Frankish friend:

> **SOURCE 28**
>
> 'When my Frankish friend decided to go home, he said to me:
> 'My friend when I leave I want you to send your son to live with me in Europe. There he can learn chivalry and wisdom from our knights. When he returns to you he will be a wise man.' This was nonsense; for even if my son were taken prisoner his captivity would be only a minor misfortune compared to bringing him up in Europe.

Usamah goes on to explain why he did not want his son educated in Europe:

SOURCE 29

The children of the Franks are taught only the arts of war, which is fitting, for Allah in his wisdom has provided them with large bodies but small minds.

Whereas my son will also study the sciences, literature, algebra, philosophy, music and history as all men do, and he might also learn about medicine.

SOURCE 30

'Non-existent money is taken from them by terrible tortures, the hard skin on their heels being cut open and peeled back to see whether perhaps they have put something under it. The cruelty of these wicked men goes even to the length that, thinking the pilgrims have eaten gold or silver, they either put scammony in their drink and force them to vomit or—and this is unspeakable—they stretch apart the coverings of all the intestines after ripping open their stomachs with a blade and reveal . . . whatever nature keeps secret.'

The Crusaders, in turn, did not think much of the Moslems. Pope Urban at Clermont described the Moslems as 'an accursed race, utterly divided from God'. And he told them to 'hasten to exterminate this vile race'. Much later Marco Polo described the Moslems as, 'wicked and treacherous'. Guibert of Nogent wrote of the Moslems' cruelty towards Christian pilgrims in Source 30.

All the sources in this section have been written from a particular viewpoint. They contain opinions as well as facts. If these sources are biased, can they still provide useful evidence to historians studying the Crusades? How can they be useful?

Discuss this question first in pairs and then share your views in a class discussion.

SOURCE 31 Saladin hanging Christians

Fulcher of Chartres who lived during the Crusades, believed the Crusades had a major effect on people living at the time (Source 32). Modern historians cannot agree whether this was so or not, as Sources 33 and 34 show.

SOURCE 32

'We who had been occidentals (westerners) have become orientals (easterners). The man who had been a Roman or Frank has here become a Galileean or a Palestinian and the man who used to live in Rheims or Chartres now finds himself a citizen of Tyre or Acre. We have already forgotten the places where we were born. (Some have) married a wife who is not from his own country, a Syrian, or even a Saracen who has become a Christian . . . He who was once a stranger here is now a native.'

Fulcher of Chartres, 1127.

SOURCE 33

'On the whole it is clear that the consequences of the Crusades for both western Christendom and Islam must be judged to be either insignificant or possibly harmful.'

The Crusades by Hans Eberhard Mayer

SOURCE 34

'The failure of the Crusades did not diminish their effect upon the future of western Europe. They had a tremendous and far reaching impact.'

The Crusades by Matthew Holden

Those historians who believe the Crusades had little effect on the West, argue that Moslem influence was the result of:

1 Contact between eastern and western traders;

2 Moslems invading parts of Europe such as Spain.

Although historians cannot agree on where the influence came from, they do agree on what areas of life were affected.

Language

Europeans took words from the Arabic, including: *damask, muslin, arsenal, sugar, syrup, lemon, admiral, almanac, alchemy.*

Trade

Italian trading cities, with their large navies, helped the Crusaders. In exchange these merchants were given special trading rights in the East. As a result, the amount of trade between the East and West greatly increased. Several new products were brought to Europe. These included: *cotton cloth, spices* (such as *cloves, nutmeg, cinnamon, musk and mace*), *sugar, apricots, lemons, damsons, melons, exotic carpets and tapestries, slippers, cosmetics* and *glass mirrors.*

Learning

In many areas of human understanding, the Moslems were far more advanced than Europeans. The West learnt much from the East about mathematics. The number system we use today comes from the Arabic system.

SOURCE 35 Origin of the modern number system

West Arabic

11th century

15th century

16th century

The Arab scholar Al-Khowarizmi wrote a book entitled 'Al-jabr . . .' (this is where Algebra comes from).

It was the East's understanding of optical science that led to the invention of the telescope. The Arabs taught the West how to separate several chemicals, including nitric and sulphuric acid. The magnetic compass, an important development for travellers, was developed in the East.

Military Tactics

There were some big changes in war tactics. The West started to make greater use of the infantry and archers and less of heavily armoured knights. There were also new ideas in castle building. Eastern castles tended to be much more complicated, with more towers, bastions and ditches. The concentric castle, with its series of walls and ditches, was an idea brought to the West from the East.

SOURCE 36 A Moslem astronomer studying a meteor

SOURCE 37 Crak des Chevaliers. The most famous crusader castle

THE END OF THE CRUSADES

SOURCE 38 The Ottoman Turks capture Constantinople.

During the 13th century the Crusades petered out. By 1280 the Crusaders found themselves sandwiched between the warring Egyptian Moslems and the Mongols (a fierce race of travelling warriors who came from North West China).

Finally, in 1291, Acre, the last christian city in the Holy Land, was captured by the Moslems.

In the 14th century any hope of restoring Jerusalem to Christianity was lost. A new Turkish race, known as the Ottoman Turks gradually began to expand its Empire. In 1453 the Ottoman Turks captured Constantinople. This marked the destruction of the Byzantine Kingdom.

ASSESSMENT

Cause and Consequence

1

The Church wanted to throw the Turks out of the Holy Land	The Crusaders wanted forgiveness for their sins	The Church wanted to unite European and Byzantine Christians
Europeans wanted to 'civilise' the Turks	The Crusaders wanted to make money	The Crusaders wanted excitement and adventure

a Which of the above six causes do you think was the most important reason for the Crusades? Explain your answer.

b Which of the above six causes do you think was the least important reason for the Crusades? Explain your answer.

2 a Make a list of the consequences or results of the Crusades.

b Divide them into short-term results—those which affected people at the time— and long-term results—those which affected people for years to come.

Evidence

3 Using the whole unit, choose 3 sources: one biased in favour of the East, one biased in favour of the West and one which is neutral. Explain your choices.

THE BLACK DEATH –
A Major Disaster

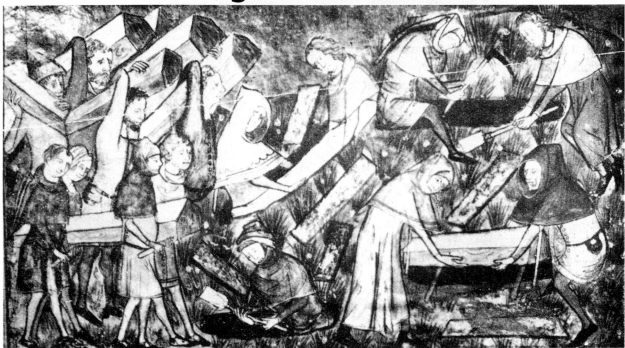

SOURCE 3 Burying the Dead

SOURCE 1

'In this year, 1348, in Melcombe Regis in the County of Dorset, a little before the feast of St John the Baptist (June 24th) two ships docked. One was from Bristol. The other was from France, and one of the sailors brought with him the terrible plague. Through him the men of the town of Melcombe were the first people in England to catch it.'

From a diary, or Chronicle, kept by a monk in the Middle Ages

THE PLAGUE THAT the monk was talking about was the Black Death. From Dorset, it spread all over Britain in 1348 and 1349. Thousands of people died: men and women, young and old, rich and poor. There seemed to be no escape.

An Italian poet, Boccaccio, who survived the Black Death wrote:

SOURCE 2

'In men and women the plague first showed itself by the appearance of swellings in the groin and armpits. Some were as large as apples or eggs. From these two parts of the body boils spread in all directions and black spots appeared on the arms or thigh.'

The boils and spots were followed by vomiting and coughing blood. People almost always died in three to five days.

AIMS

From these descriptions, modern doctors can tell that this disease that struck Britain and Europe was what we now call Bubonic Plague. In this unit we shall be looking at what people thought about the Black Death at the time. This will tell us a good deal about what people of the 14th century thought about the serious matters of life and death.

The Black Death was an EPIDEMIC. That is, it brought about the deaths of large numbers of people all over the country. It was the greatest NATURAL DISASTER of the Middle Ages, far more serious than any MAN-MADE DISASTER, such as a war. Even those who survived found that their lives were changed by it. In the second part of the unit, we shall look at how life for the people of Britain was changed by the disaster. We shall explore the LONG-TERM AND SHORT-TERM RESULTS of the Black Death.

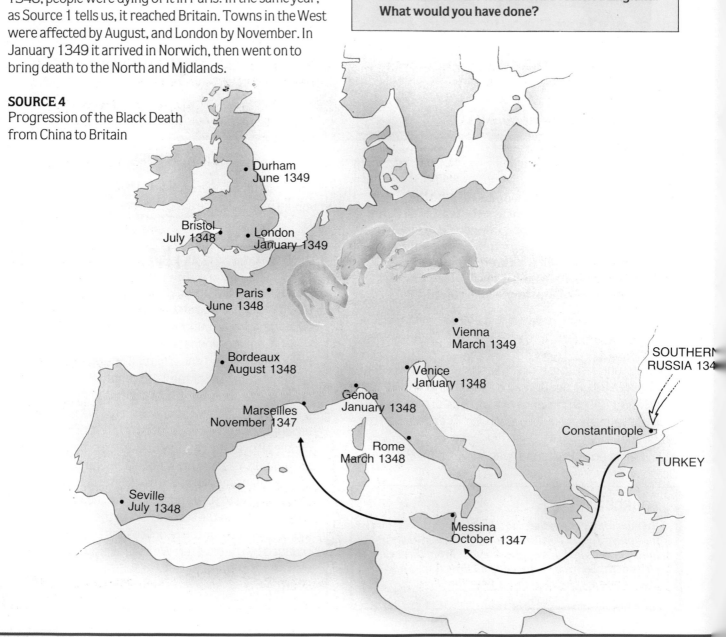

WHERE DID THE PLAGUE COME FROM?

In 1894 scientists discovered the cause of bubonic plague. It came from a germ which lived on fleas that lived on black rats. When the rats died, the fleas moved to live on humans, and the plague germ got into their blood. As we saw in unit 6, towns were crowded, dirty places. There was a lot of rubbish about for rats to feed on. Most people had fleas anyway, so they had no idea that it was the fleas that carried the plague germs.

The Black Death seems to have started in China in 1334. It spread westwards along trade routes and reached southern Russia in 1346. By late 1347 it was in Sicily, and then in Marseilles. Look at Source 4. By June 1348, people were dying of it in Paris. In the same year, as Source 1 tells us, it reached Britain. Towns in the West were affected by August, and London by November. In January 1349 it arrived in Norwich, then went on to bring death to the North and Midlands.

1. Trace a rough copy of Source 4. Draw arrows on your map to show the progression of the Black Death.
2. When do you think it reached the place where *you* live?
3. Your map is now a map of the trade routes of Europe. Why do you think the Black Death followed the trade routes?
4. How did it cross the sea?
5. Why did it affect towns first, and worst?
6. Join up into small groups. Discuss how you would have felt in the summer of 1348, when you heard that the Black Death had reached England. What would you have done?

SOURCE 4
Progression of the Black Death from China to Britain

Durham
June 1349

Bristol
July 1348

London
January 1349

Paris
June 1348

Vienna
March 1349

Bordeaux
August 1348

Venice
January 1348

Genoa
January 1348

Marseilles
November 1347

SOUTHERN
RUSSIA 134

Constantinople

TURKEY

Rome
March 1348

Seville
July 1348

Messina
October 1347

The Black Death frightened people so much because they did not know what caused it or how to cure it. It was a mystery killer. Obviously, they couldn't just do nothing. All sorts of ideas were put forward about how to avoid the plague. They tell us a great deal about how people thought in the Middle Ages.

What did people think were the causes?

The most popular theory for the cause of the Black Death was put forward by a French doctor, Guy de Chauliac, in 1363. Source 5 explains his theory.

SOURCE 5

'There were two causes of the Plague, one general and one particular. The general cause was the close position of the three great planets, Saturn, Jupiter and Mars. This had taken place in 1345, on March 24th. Such a coming together of the planets is always a sign of wonderful, terrible or violent things to come.'

'The particular cause of the disease in each person was the state of the body—bad digestion, weakness or blockage. For this reason, people died.'

1 What does Source 5 tell us about what people knew at that time?
2 What does it tell us about what people believed at that time?

ACTIVITY

Below are nine ideas put forward at the time about how to avoid the plague.

In groups, draw up a table like this one:

No use at all	Would cure the plague	Would help avoid catching the plague

As you read through the ideas, put each one (1–9) in the column which you think best describes the result it would have.

1 Avoid breathing in germs when with a plague victim (Source 6).

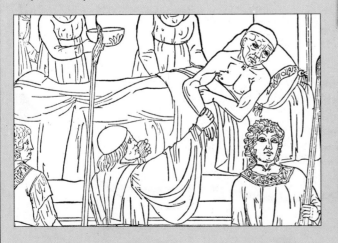

2 Sit next to a blazing fire (as the Pope did) right through the hot summer of 1348.

3 Attack foreigners and people of a different religion. Twenty thousand Jews were burnt to death in Strasbourg, in 1348.

4 Live in a house sheltered from the wind and keep the windows closed.

5 SOURCE 7

'The swellings should be softened with figs and cooked onions mixed with yeast and butter. When they are open they should be treated with the cure for ulcers. Towards the end of the plague, I developed a fever with a swelling in the groin. I was ill near on six weeks. When the swelling had ripened and had been treated in the way I prescribed, I escaped, by God's grace.'

Guy de Chauliac

6 SOURCE 8

'You are to make sure that all the human excrement and other filth lying in the streets of the city is removed. You are to cause the city to be cleaned from all bad smells so that no more people will die from such smells.'

Letter from King Edward III to the Lord Mayor of London, 1349

7 SOURCE 9 Flagellant procession

These people travelled about whipping each other. They believed that the Black Death was God's punishment. They punished themselves in order to beg God for forgiveness.

8 SOURCE 10

'Toads should be thoroughly dried in the sun. They should be laid on the boil. The toad will swell and draw out the poison of the plague to its own body. When it is full, it should be thrown away and a new one applied.'

A doctor's advice

Now discuss your results.
- You've probably put some ideas in the first column. If they were no use at all, why do you think people took notice of them?
- You've probably put some ideas in the third column. People in 1348–9 did not know the real cause of the Black Death, or how it spread. How did they come up with ideas which were actually some help? Share your answers to these questions in a class discussion.

9 Plague motto: 'Quick-far-late.' That is, go away quickly, go far away, don't come back until late.

THE PLAGUE STRIKES

The Black Death was worse in towns and cities. London, the biggest city in Britain, obviously had most deaths. Two hundred people per day were dying at the peak of the plague. By then they were not being buried in coffins as in Source 3. The bodies were just tipped into huge pits. Two new cemeteries had to be made outside the city.

The Italian poet, Boccaccio, described how people behaved in Source 11.

People were used to death in the Middle Ages. Babies often died, people were old at 45 and a poor harvest meant starvation. But the Black Death was far worse.

SOURCE 11

'Some shut themselves away and waited for death, others rioted from tavern to tavern. The sickness fell upon all classes without distinction. The rich passed out of this world without a single person to comfort them. The poor fell sick by the thousand and most of them died. The terror was such that brother even fled from brother, wife from husband, yea, the mother from her own child.'

SOURCE 12 Dance of Death

Pictures of death dancing with people were often made at this time.

> 1 **What sort of people are shown here?**
> 2 **What does this tell us about who got the Plague and who didn't?**

It is difficult to know exactly how many died. Nowadays every death has to be registered. There were no such registers in the Middle Ages. How can historians find out? The Church was the only organisation to keep accurate records. Bishops noted down when a new priest was appointed to a parish church. In many areas half the churches had new priests in 1348 or 1349. In some monasteries nearly all the monks died. Probably the death rate in the Church was particularly high. Priests visited the sick to comfort them, so were likely to catch the Plague. Once the Black Death got into a monastery it would easily spread to all the monks. Historians estimate that about one third or more of the population of England and Wales died. This would be over one million people.

Number round the class 1–2–3, 1–2–3 and so on. All the No 2 people stand up and walk out of the room. What does the class look like? Did your friend go out? How did you feel if you were left behind? How did you feel if you had to walk out?

RESULTS OF THE BLACK DEATH

Historians try to decide what the results are of a big event, like the Black Death. Some results are obvious at once—these we call short-term results. Others take longer to appear—these we call long-term results.

Short-term results

1 In the towns the busy streets were deserted. Houses were full of dead bodies waiting to be buried. Trade was interrupted and those who had survived made a living in any way they could. Many people were in a state of shock.

2 In the villages, the streets and houses were empty, too. Sometimes there were not enough people alive to look after the animals, and they died too. Crops rotted in the fields.

3 In some places so few people were left in a village that they abandoned it completely.

SOURCE 13 Aerial photograph of a deserted village in Buckinghamshire. You can see the streets and lanes of the village as marks in the grass. Sometimes villagers tried to work the land of a village for a few years, and then gave up. Deserted villages are both a short-term and a long-term result of the Black Death.

Long-term results

Bubonic Plague stayed in Britain for a long time. It was ENDEMIC. It was never as serious as the Black Death, but people continued to die from it. As the graph in Source 14 shows, the population took about 200 years to return to the level of 1348. The fact that there were fewer people had a big effect on prices, wages and labour services.

SOURCE 14 Graph showing rapid decrease in population

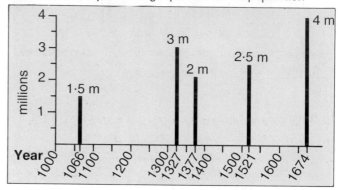

1 Prices. Before the Black Death a horse could be sold for £2.00. Afterwards, with a lower population, would it cost more or less?
It cost less—only 6s 8d (33p)—because there were plenty of horses to go round now.

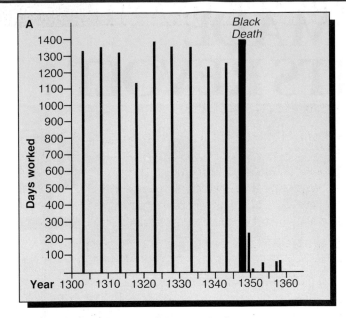

SOURCE 15 A Number of days worked

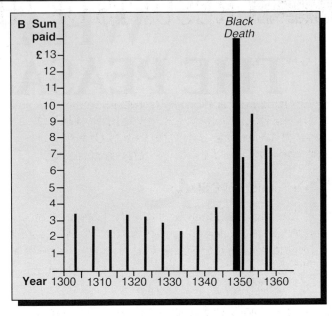

B Wages paid in the village of Cuxham, Oxfordshire

2 **Wages and labour services.** As we saw in Unit 6, most of the work on the land was done as labour service by the peasants. They had to work for their lord for so many days per year, in return for their own land. Some lords might hire a few labourers to do some work as well, paying them about 4d (1½p) a day. You can see from Source 15 that the lord used to receive about 1,200 days' worth of work per year before the Black Death. His wages bill was about £3.00 per year.

> a How many days' work, at 1½p per day, can the lord buy for £3?
> b What happened to labour services after the Black Death?
> c Can you work out why labour services fell?

The lords had to find someone to work their land. Those people who survived the disaster realised that they were in demand, and asked for higher wages. Sometimes the lord paid as much as 10d (4p) per day, with free food and drink, just to get the work done.

Those peasants who should have done labour services began to refuse. Why should they do a day's work for nothing when they could get 10d (4p)? Thus the whole way of life on the land began to change.

3 **Attitudes.** For peasants who survived the Black Death these were good times. Prices were low and wages were high. They were not afraid to stand up for themselves against the barons and lords, the Church, even the King. Perhaps the disaster had something to do with this: so many had died that those who were left felt special in some way. Once they had faced death, and escaped it, why should they be frightened of anything?

ASSESSMENT

Empathy

You live in the village of Imchester. It is 1350. The Plague has died down and you have survived, although the priest, the Lady of the Manor, and many villagers, including members of your own family, have died.

Write six entries for your diary over the past 2 years; one from before the Black Death arrived, three while it was going on, and two since it has ended. Remember that when people write the diaries they do not know what is going to happen next. Look back over the work you have done on what people thought about the Black Death, its causes, and how to avoid it. End the last entry with your feelings now it is all over.

WHAT MADE THE PEASANTS REVOLT ?

SOURCE 1 John Ball leading the Peasants' Revolt. This illustration was made in about 1460.

IN 1381, THOUSANDS of peasants in southern England joined up and marched to London. The King, Richard II, was a boy of 14. For some days he could do nothing, and the rebels took over London. The REBELLION ended when their leader was killed. It was the first of several great rebellions that took place in Britain over the next 300 years. The last was the great Civil War which you will read about in Book 2.

1 In Source 1 find: John Ball, his followers, the City of London, the King's men.
2 The picture shows the peasants well-armed and wearing armour. Is this likely to be true?
3 In pairs suggest reasons why the peasants rebelled in 1381. Make a note of your reasons. Talk about your ideas with the rest of the class. When you have finished reading the unit check back to see what your original ideas were.

AIMS

In this unit we shall look at the reasons why this first great Peasants' Revolt of 1381 took place. Why did thousands of ordinary men in villages in Essex and Kent leave their homes and march to London? What drove them to it? What were their motives? These are obviously very difficult questions, and historians can only suggest the reasons. Some reasons go back a long way, like the change in attitudes to life after the Black Death noted in the last unit. These are long-term reasons. Some arise out of the events of the moment: something happens that leads a person to say 'Right, that's it, that's enough!' These are short-term reasons. Look out for long-term and short-term causes of the revolt in the account that follows.

The Statute of Labourers, 1351

The lords were angry because the peasants refused to do labour services (see page 115). They also disliked having to pay high wages to get their work done.

At that time, Parliament met rarely. It only met when there were serious issues to discuss which affected the whole country. This was one of those times. The Members of Parliament were not elected by the people, as they are now. They were chosen by the lords from among themselves. They passed a law, the Statute of Labourers, which tried to put things back to the way that they were before the Black Death.

> ### SOURCE 2
> 'Workers are idle, and not willing to work after the plague without excessive wages ... Therefore, these servants should have to work for the usual wages of 1347, or five or six years before. Workers refusing to work in such a way should be punished by imprisonment.
>
> Thus carters, ploughmen, shepherds, swineherds and all other workers shall take the payments they received in 1347 . . . They are to be hired for the whole year, not by the day . . . None to pay a mower of meadows more than 5d (2p) an acre or 5d a day. Also that none take more than 2½d (1p) for threshing a quarter of wheat or rye . . .'
>
> Statute of Labourers, 1351 (adapted)

In the next few years many people were taken to court for taking higher wages, or for offering higher wages to labourers.

> ### SOURCE 3
> 'John Julian of Newnton, William Smyth of Laughton and Robert Joy of the same place received in 1373 8d (3½p) an acre for every acre mowed by them; whereas by the Statute of Labourers they should have taken 5d (2p) and no more.'

> 'John Gale on the Thursday after Whitsun, 1374 enticed John Donney, servant of Walter Hardegray of Edlyngton, away from Walter's service; and took him in and hired him at his own service at Edlyngton, giving him for his yearly wage 6s 8d (33p) and his food, as well as other goods, against the form of the Statute of Labourers.'
>
> Justices in the County of Lincolnshire, 1373–4

1. What had John Julian, William Smyth and Robert Joy done which was against the law?
2. What had John Gale done which was against the law?
3. Why do you think these offences took place?
4. Do you think the Statute of Labourers was fair? Explain your answer.

Source 3 shows that the efforts of lords to hold down wages and keep things as they were before did not succeed. Most peasants hated the Statute of Labourers. They wanted to be free to work for what they could get. Some peasants ran away from their villages. They could go to a town, or another village to find work. Good wages could be earned, and not too many questions asked. Some lords agreed to free their peasants from labour services and charge rents in money. Others refused. Among those who stuck hardest to the old ways were abbots and bishops. This brought bitter criticism of the Church from the peasants.

John Ball

Some poorer priests agreed with the peasants. They attacked the leaders of the Church for being rich and idle. They also criticised the nobles and lords. They pointed out the big difference between the hard-working life of the poor and the easy, luxurious life of the rich.

One such poor priest was John Ball. He was banned from preaching in churches, so he preached in market-places and fields—anywhere that people could gather to listen. He said that the lords lived off the sweat of the common people. In his sermons he referred to the simple life led by Adam and Eve in the Garden of Eden.

Like many Bible stories, this was often illustrated in paintings on the inside walls of churches. Ball's hearers would understand what he meant when he said:

'When Adam delved (dug) and Eve span,
Who was then the gentleman?'

This became a kind of 'slogan' for all those who criticised the richer classes.

> 1 What did John Ball's message mean?
> 2 In 1381 John Ball was arrested and put in prison at Maidstone by the Archbishop of Canterbury. Why did the Archbishop want him out of the way?

Taxation

Nowadays everyone who has a job pays taxes. To try and be fair, the system is arranged so that people pay according to the amount they earn.

In the fourteenth century, tax of any kind was quite unusual. People did not expect to pay tax every year. In the 1370s the government needed money to pay for a war against France. In 1377 they asked for a groat (4d, or 1½p) from everyone over 15 years of age in the country. Then in 1379 they asked for another groat from everyone, and in 1380 three groats. These were called 'Poll Taxes'—a tax on every person, regardless of their income.

Peasants became angry for three reasons. They thought the taxes were coming round too often. They thought a Poll Tax was unfair. They thought the amount asked for was far too high. Lots of people tried to avoid paying. When the tax collectors arrived in the village they would hide, or lie about how many adults there were in their family.

In 1381, the government sent round commissioners to check on everybody in order to stop all the tax-dodging. The people thought that they were being asked for another tax, and the Peasants' Revolt began.

> Look at the three reasons given above why the peasants were angry about the taxes. Do you think any of their complaints were justified?

SOURCE 4 A medieval groat

THE REVOLT

In May 1381 there were riots in several villages in Essex when the commissioners arrived. The same thing happened in Kent. There the rebels took the castle at Rochester and marched to Maidstone. Here they chose Wat Tyler as their leader and forced the keeper of the prison to release John Ball.

On June 11 they turned to march to London, arriving at Blackheath, five miles outside the City, in only two days. They picked up supporters from every village along the way, armed with bows, axes, hedge-cutters and scythes. (They were certainly not wearing full armour, like the picture in Source 1, which only knights could afford.) They attacked tax-collectors' and lawyers' houses. Not much damage was done, but they burnt documents of the manor which recorded what rights lords had over them.

Meanwhile, the rebels from Essex had also marched to London, and camped at Mile End, just outside the city. The two groups of rebels were certainly in contact with each other. It is difficult for us to tell, but there may have been over 50,000 of them altogether.

SOURCE 5 Map showing the peasants' attack on London

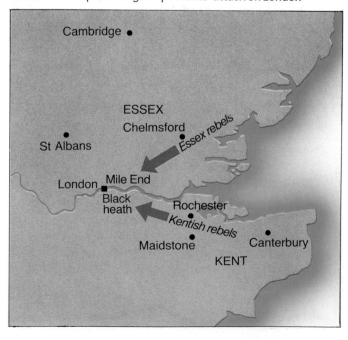

John Ball spoke to the Kentish rebels at Blackheath:

SOURCE 6

'My good friends, things cannot go well in England until everyone is equal. Then there shall be neither slaves nor lords, and lords be no more masters than we are. How ill they treat us! Are we not all descended from the same ancestors, Adam and Eve?

They are dressed in velvet and other rich clothes, decorated with ermine, while we are forced to wear rags. They have wines, spices and fine bread, while we have only black bread and scraps from the straw. When we drink it must be water. They have handsome houses, while we must brave the wind and rain to labour in the field. We are called slaves, and if we do not perform our services we are beaten.

We have no one to whom we can complain who is willing to hear us. Let us go to the King and argue with him. He is young and from him we may get a good answer. If not, we ourselves must try to put things right.'

From Froissart's *Chronicle*

1 The peasants of 1381 were not allowed to vote. (There were no councils and no trade unions.) Who did they decide to complain to?
2 What does John Ball say they must do if that person won't help them?
3 What effect do you think this sermon of John Ball's would have had on the rebels at Blackheath?
4 Froissart was alive at the time, but we do not know if he was there. Do you think this source is very reliable? How should an historian look on this source?

ACTIVITY

Get into groups of four.
Imagine you are Wat Tyler's advisers. You have just arrived at Blackheath, outside London.

a What problems do you have to deal with?

b What are you afraid of?

c What do you hope to do?

1 Discuss these questions in your group, and come to a group decision as to what you will do next.
2 Compare your decisions with the other groups in the class and explain clearly why you came to them.
3 Compare your ideas with what the rebels actually did as described next.

The Revolt Reaches London

On June 12 the King, Richard II, and his advisers travelled down the river by barge to meet the rebels. As the King came to Greenwich, the excited rebels were shouting and yelling so much that his advisers thought it was too dangerous to land. He returned to the Tower.

The rebels then began to attack places outside the city walls. The Kentish rebels released the prisoners from the Marshalsea prison, in Southwark (see Source 7). The Essex rebels attacked Lambeth Palace, home of the hated Archbishop and Chancellor, Simon of Sudbury.

Early on June 13 they got into the city of London. Either the people of the city agreed with the rebels, or the Mayor was too frightened to try and stop them. The Kentish rebels came across London Bridge. The Essex rebels were let in through Aldgate.

The rebels needed food and drink badly, which the people of London supplied. They then attacked the homes of the men they most hated: Sir Robert Hales, the Royal Treasurer, blamed for the Poll Taxes, and the King's uncle, John of Gaunt, who supported the war against France. Hales' house was burnt. John of Gaunt's huge palace at the Savoy, in the Strand, was blown up. At this stage the rebels were well-disciplined and did not steal anything.

The King and his advisers were trapped in the Tower. There was no police force, and no army large enough to defeat the rebels. His only hope was to offer to talk to them and persuade them to go home quietly.

When the King met the rebels at Mile End on June 14 he granted pardon and freedom to all the peasants from Essex and Hertfordshire. At this, many of the rebels from these counties went home. He also promised that all traitors would be seized and executed, if they were guilty.

Some of the rebels took this as permission to hunt down those royal officials whom they hated. Simon of Sudbury and Sir Robert Hales were both killed, along with many others. For the next two days the rebels went on the rampage in London. Many were drunk, and lots of people were killed.

The Death of Tyler

On June 15, the King met Wat Tyler again, at Smithfield. It is difficult to know exactly what took place there, as all the accounts were written by either royal or church officials. They are, therefore, biased against the rebels. Hardly any of the rebels could write so no account of their point of view exists.

Many of the royal officials were furious at what was happening in London. Perhaps they planned to kill Tyler. Tyler demanded that all men should be free, all church property should be given to the people, and there should be only one bishop in the whole country. Some accounts say he refused to take his hat off to the King, and spat on the ground. After a scuffle with one of the royal followers Tyler drew a dagger. The Mayor of London then struck him with his sword, and one of the royal knights killed him. The rebels began to fit arrows to their bows, and it looked as if the royal party would be massacred. At this dangerous moment Richard rode forward, calling, 'I will be your leader'. The rebels, always loyal to the King, followed him. Almost alone, he led them out of the city. He agreed to their demands and most rebels began to go home.

SOURCE 7 Peasant routes to London

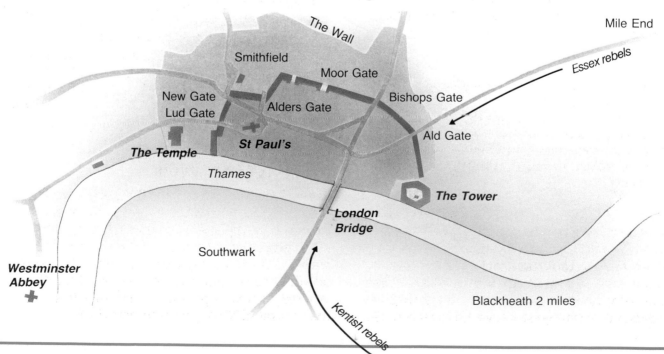

SOURCE 8 The killing of Wat Tyler, from another of the illustrations to Froissart's *Chronicle* made in 1460. There are really two incidents in the same picture here and King Richard appears twice. (Painters quite often did this in the Middle Ages.) On the left the Mayor of London is about to strike Wat Tyler, who is talking to the King. On the right King Richard II goes over to talk to the rebels.

1 Is this source a primary or secondary source on the Peasants' Revolt?
2 In what ways does it disagree with other statements already made in this unit?
3 How could you check the accuracy of the picture?
4 Is this picture any use at all to a historian of the Revolt?

The Mayor of London had collected a large force of armed men, and any rebels remaining in the city were driven out. All Londoners had to promise loyalty to the King. Over the next few weeks, royal forces went into Essex and Kent. All the promises Richard had made were withdrawn. 'Villeins you were and villeins you shall remain', he told the Essex peasants at Waltham Forest. All over Essex rebel leaders were rounded up and hanged. Then the same thing happened in Kent. John Ball was hanged and beheaded at St Albans on July 15. His body was cut into four pieces and sent to the four ends of England.

There were other rebellions in the summer of 1381. The abbey at Bury St Edmunds was attacked, and the prior hunted down and killed. The abbey at St Albans was broken into, as was Norwich Castle. At Cambridge the university was attacked. However, by the autumn it was all over. Only the peasants' vivid memories, and the bodies rotting on the gibbets, reminded them of the day when they had taken over the capital of England.

Results of the Revolt

The Peasants' Revolt was not a total failure, though. The King and the lords knew better than to provoke similar trouble again. The hated Poll Tax was never repeated. Efforts were made to keep wages down, but they never really succeeded. The shortage of workers was bound to bring the end of labour services in the long run. Within a hundred years all the peasants had been granted their freedom. By 1500 there were no more villeins.

ASSESSMENT

The Black Death	Statute of Labourers, 1351	John Ball's sermon
1380 Poll Tax	The French Wars	Wat Tyler's leadership

1 a Choose three of the items from this table which you think were the *most* important causes of the Peasants' Revolt. Explain your choice.
  b Choose one item from the table which was an important short-term cause of the Peasants' Revolt.
  c Choose two items from the table which were important long-term causes of the Peasants' Revolt.
  d Add one other cause of the Peasants' Revolt which is not in this table, and explain why you have chosen it.

   Discuss this question first in a group.

2 a Think of an experiment you have done recently in your science lesson. What happened? Why did it happen? Do you think the same thing would happen if you did the experiment again tomorrow?
  b Now think about the Peasants' Revolt. Was there one main reason for it? Why are the other reasons important? Do you think all rebellions have the same causes?
  c Now, on your own, write a short paragraph saying how explanations of why things happen seem to be different in history and in science.

TIMELINE

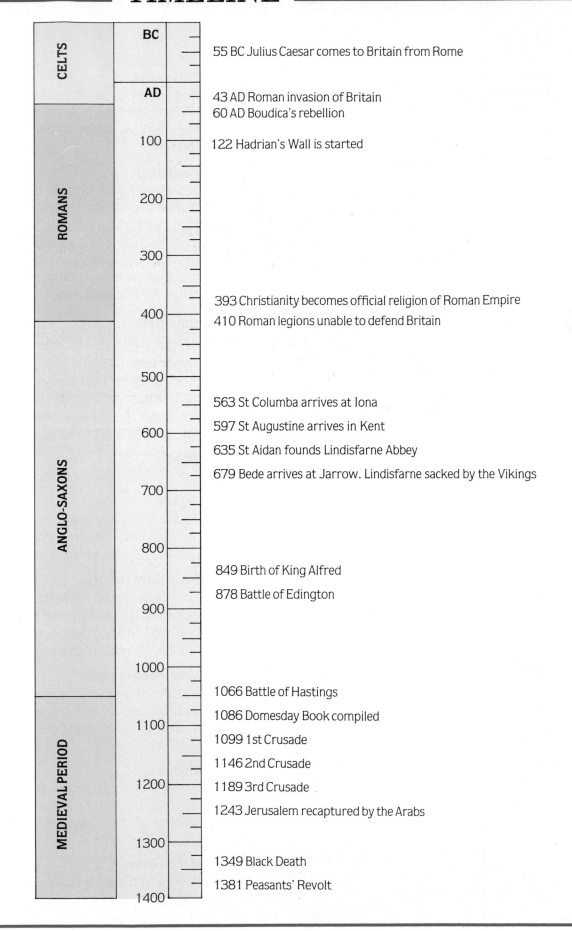

CELTS

ROMANS

ANGLO-SAXONS

MEDIEVAL PERIOD

BC

AD

100
200
300
400
500
600
700
800
900
1000
1100
1200
1300
1400

55 BC Julius Caesar comes to Britain from Rome

43 AD Roman invasion of Britain
60 AD Boudica's rebellion

122 Hadrian's Wall is started

393 Christianity becomes official religion of Roman Empire
410 Roman legions unable to defend Britain

563 St Columba arrives at Iona

597 St Augustine arrives in Kent

635 St Aidan founds Lindisfarne Abbey

679 Bede arrives at Jarrow. Lindisfarne sacked by the Vikings

849 Birth of King Alfred

878 Battle of Edington

1066 Battle of Hastings

1086 Domesday Book compiled

1099 1st Crusade

1146 2nd Crusade

1189 3rd Crusade

1243 Jerusalem recaptured by the Arabs

1349 Black Death

1381 Peasants' Revolt

Archaeologist
Person who studies the distant past usually by digging for remains, for example, buildings, pottery or other finds.

Bailey
The outer walled enclosure of a castle.

Baptism
A religous ceremony which makes someone a Christian.

Bias
Holding a particular point of view. 'Bias' can often be unconscious – writers for example can think they are being fair when in fact they are expressing their own opinion; but bias can also be deliberate, for example trying to give a one-sided version of an event.

Bishop
Someone responsible for organising the Church in a particular large area, called a *diocese*.

Bubonic Plague
A fatal disease carried by parasites.

Christianity
Religion of those who follow the teachings of Jesus Christ. They believe him to be the Son of God.

Church
Either a building where Christians worship God *or* the organisation of all the people who belong to a certain Christian faith.

Concentric
A castle with two or more sets of walls, one inside the other. The outer walls were usually lower than the inner walls allowing archers from both walls to fire out.

Diocese
A large area which is governed by a *bishop*.

Empathy
Ability to understand the values, attitudes and beliefs of another person or group of people.

Epidemic
A particular disease which spreads rapidly and affects large numbers of people.

Evidence
A historical *source* is anything left from the past – a book, a letter, a photograph, a painting, a house, an object. If we look at it carefully and ask the right questions, a source may give us *evidence* about what we are studying.

Excavated
Dug away to show what lies under the ground, for example, the foundations of a house, the ground plan of a town, and any objects left behind by the people who lived there.

Feudalism
Word used for the organisation of medieval society. The important people of the country were given land by the king. In return for this they had certain duties such as governing the area they had been given and helping the king in time of war by providing soldiers. Less important people belonged to their lords, and worked for them, in return for their protection.

Holy War
A war fought in the name of a religion.

Hypocaust
A Roman central heating system. The floor of the house was raised about ½ metre on small columns. A furnace at one side of the house sent hot air into this space under the floor, so heating the rooms.

Jihad
A religious war fought by Moslems against non-Moslems.

Legend
A story often passed down by word of mouth concerning the history of a nation or group of people. Legends usually contain a mixture of fact, truth and exaggeration.

Long-term results
The effects of an event which takes place a long time after that event. For example, the long-term result of the Black Death of 1349 was that the feudal system was gradually replaced by a system of wages for workers.

Man-made disaster
A sudden or great misfortune that is the result of actions taken by people. For example, the escape of radio-active waste from the Russian power station at Chernobyl in 1986 was a man-made disaster.

Medieval
This means the Middle Ages, and usually refers to the time from the end of the Roman Empire to the Renaissance. Approximately the 5th century AD to 1400 AD.

Mercenaries
Soldiers who will fight for any country provided they are paid.

Middle Ages
Name given to period of history roughly between the dates of the 5th century AD to AD 1400.

Mosaic
A pattern or picture made of small pieces of coloured tile, used to decorate floors, especially by the Romans.

Motte
Mound, often man-made, which forms the highest point of a castle and on which the *keep* is built.

Myth
A traditional story perhaps involving heroes, heroines, gods, goddesses, giants or demons. Myths are often told as a way of explaining mysteries such as the creation of the world.

Nation-state
A group of people living in one area who govern themselves with the same laws and the same way.

Natural disaster
A sudden or great misfortune which is the result of a storm, flood or widespread disease.

Pagan
Not belonging to a certain religion or having religious beliefs.

Parish
A small area which has its own church and clergymen.

Pope
The Head of the Roman Catholic Church.

Priest
Someone with the special job of worshipping God and organising the Church in a small area, like a village or *parish*.

Primary Evidence
Evidence gained from sources which come from the period being studied. For example, eyewitness accounts, pictures taken or drawn at the time, objects such as pottery which come from the period are all examples of primary sources of evidence. They can be thought of as the raw materials for the historian which are used to construct the secondary account of what happened.

Rebellion
An organised uprising against the government of a country. It aims to change the policies of the government or overthrow it.

Saint
A person whom after death the Church sees as being exceptionally holy.

Secondary evidence
Evidence gained from accounts of events put together at a later date by historians. For example, an account of the Norman Conquest written in 1988 would provide secondary evidence for the Conquest.

Short-term results
The immediate effects of an event. For example the short-term result of the Black Death of 1349 was that about one third of the population of England died and there was a shortage of labour.

Succeed
To take the place of somebody else, for example a king.

Synod
A council or parliament representing the whole of a church.

Tribe
A group of people led by a chief. A tribe usually claims to have a common ancestor, and is made up of a number of families.

Witan
Council of important men who advised the Anglo-Saxon kings. The word 'witan' is old English for 'men of knowledge'.

SKILLS GRID

This grid tells you what you will learn to do in each unit in this book.

	Historical Ideas	Ways of understanding history				
		Role of the individual	Cause and consequence	Similarity and difference	Change	Continuity
UNIT 1 **Finding out about . . . The Romans in Britain**	Civilisation			✓		
UNIT 2 **Anglo-Saxons: Settlement and Church**	Settlement Church Pagan Civilisation					
UNIT 3 **King Alfred – The Great?**	King Government Myth/Legend Hero	✓				
UNIT 4 **The Norman Invasion and Conquest**	Invasion Conquest Feudalism		✓			
UNIT 5 **The Rise and Fall of the Castle**	Baron Feudalism Government				✓	✓
UNIT 6 **Village Life – Town Life**	Apprentice Market Town Village			✓		
UNIT 7 **The Crusades – Clashes between Moslems and Christians**	Crusade Culture		✓			
UNIT 8 **The Black Death – A Major Disaster**	Plague Epidemic					
UNIT 9 **What made the Peasants Revolt?**	Revolt		✓			

	Evidence Skills			Empathy	Chronology	
Comprehension	Primary and Secondary sources	Making use of evidence	Bias and reliability			
		✓			✓	UNIT 1 **Finding out about . . . The Romans in Britain**
	✓	✓			✓	UNIT 2 **Anglo-Saxons: Settlement and Church**
						UNIT 3 **King Alfred – The Great?**
		✓	✓			UNIT 4 **The Norman Invasion and Conquest**
					✓	UNIT 5 **The Rise and Fall of the Castle**
				✓		UNIT 6 **Village Life – Town Life**
✓						UNIT 7 **The Crusades – Clashes between Moslems and Christians**
				✓		UNIT 8 **The Black Death – A Major Disaster**
						UNIT 9 **What made the Peasants Revolt?**

ACKNOWLEDGEMENTS

The publishers would like to thank the following for permission to reproduce photographs.

t(Top), b(Bottom), r(Right), l(Left), m(Middle)

Aerofilms p40(b) P80, Airfotos p64(tr) p93, Aldus Archives p65, Alecto Historical Editions p78, Ashmolean Museum, Oxford p43 p46 (br) Ancient Art and Architecture Collection p4 (tl and tr) p31 (ml) p35 p37 (br) p82 (bl) p83 (tr) p101 (bl), Bath Museum Service p16 (tl) Batsford p95 (b), BBC Hulton Picture Library p85 (tr) p104 p109 p112, Bede Monastery Museum p31 (r), Bibliotheque Nationale, Paris p97 p105 p108, Bibliotheque Royale, Bruxelles p90 (l), Bodleian Library, Oxford p33 (br) p84 (t) p89 (bl), British Library p23 (bl) p34 p76 (t & m) p77 p81(t) p90 (tr) p92 p100 (mr) p116 p121, Trustees of British Museum p4 (bl & mr) p17 (mr) p23(t), p27 p28 p36 p39 (ml) p118 (t), Boyer: History of Mathematics (John Wiley) p106, Cadw: Welsh Historic Monuments p16 (bl) p67 (b) p75 (br), by permission of the Syndics of Cambridge University Library p50 (l), Central Press p63 (b), Colchester and Essex Museum Service p17 (ml) p25 (b), Corpus Christie Colege p50 (r), Dean and Chapter of Durham Cathedral p45 (b), English Heritage p2 (b) p5 p16 (br) p19 p66 (t) p67 (t) p69 p70, Essex Planning Office p64 (br), Fotomas Index p84 p64 (tl), Giraudon p79 (r), Grosvenor Museum, Chester p12 p21, Denis Hardley pl (t), Heart of England Tourist Board p87 (m), Resort Services Department, Harrowgate Borough Council p87 (t), Michael Holford p48 p49 (t) p51 p53 p57 p59 p66 (b) p75, Illustrated London News p30, A F Kersting p33 (t) p61 (tr & tl) p29 (tr) p107 (b), Keystone Collection p37 (t), Mansell Collection p15 (t, bl) p17 (t) p96 p98 p102 p111 p113, Museum of London p15 (br) p17 (mtl), Ewan Moore p75, National Trust Photographic Library p73 (b) p74 (br) p90, Norfolk Museum Service (Norwich Castle Museum) p22. Norman Conquest by M Reeves (Longmans) p60, Dr P J Reynolds, Butser Ancient Farm p4 (b), Rochdale Libraries and Arts Department p18, Rowleys House Museum, Shrewsbury p2 (tl), The Royal Library, Windsor p74 (tl), Scottish Office jp73 (t), Society of Antiquaries p13, Alan Sorrell p63 (t), St Albans Museum Service p14, Sutcliffe Gallery p95 (t), Trinity College, Dublin p71, Regina Tombstone: from the Collection at Arbeia Roman Fort South Shields. Reproduced by permission of Tyne and Wear Museum Service p20, University of Cambridge: Committee for Aerial Photography p1 (b) p63 (m) p88 p114 (bl), Universitetets Oldsaksamling p39 (tl & tr), Viscount De L'Isle p72, Warburg Institute p64 (bl), Walters Art Gallery, Baltimore p62, Wayland Picture Library p107 (t) Welholme Galleries (WER Hallgarth Collection, Great Grimsby Borough Council) p78, York Archaeological Trust p41 (b) p42, Yorkshire Museum p2.

Cover photographs: Universitetets Oldsaksamling p39 (tl)
Bodleian Library p84 (m)
Bibliotheque Nationale p108 (b)

Every effort has been made to contact owners of copyright material but if any have been inadvertently overlooked the publishers will be pleased to make the necessary arrangements at the first opportunity.

Collins Educational, 8 Grafton Street, London W1X 3LA

© Christopher Culpin, David Linsell, Martin Booth

First published 1988

Reprinted 1989 (twice)

ISBN 0 00 3272206 6

Designed by Robert Wheeler Associates

Artwork by Tony Garrett, Len Day, Ray Burrows, Robert Wheeler

Typeset by CG Graphics Services, Tring

Printed and bound by G. Canale & C. s.p.a., Italy